AIR

The Earth series traces the historical significance and cultural history of natural phenomena. Written by experts who are passionate about their subject, titles in the series bring together science, art, literature, mythology, religion and popular culture, exploring and explaining the planet we inhabit in new and exciting ways.

Series editor: Daniel Allen

Air

Peter Adey

REAKTION BOOKS

For Hayley

Published by
Reaktion Books Ltd
33 Great Sutton Street
London EC1V 0DX, UK
www.reaktionbooks.co.uk

First published 2014

Printed and bound in China

A catalogue record for this book is available from the British Library

ISBN 978 1 78023 256 0

CONTENTS

Introduction

Air is 78 per cent nitrogen, 21 per cent oxygen, 0.96 per cent argon and 0.4 per cent other gases and elements. This is roughly the composition of air and it is something in which we all have a stake. It is something that we need, so vital to our existence. Despite its lack of appearance, it is not as if the air is left untouched by us. In fact, each human uses around 360 litres per hour. We must consume air all the time. And so even if we do not like to think about it very often, the air is deserving of our attention.

Each breath is about half a litre of the stuff. We push and pull it in and out of our bodies, infusing our blood with the oxygen from the air while expelling air as exhaust, as breath, belch, burp, fart or speech. Taking in air – inhaling – expands the chest cavity in a move performed by the diaphragm, which can contract and expand. This increase to your thoracic volume generates the negative pressure gradient allowing air to fill your lungs with what they need. What we most need, however, is that 21 per cent oxygen which is diffused by the lungs into the bloodstream. What comes out, the air that exits the body, is different. The body has pulled the oxygen out of the air and returned it with an increase in carbon dioxide, water vapour and a little bit of heat.

So we could say that our bodies are essentially walking air filters, especially for plants which like to absorb the carbon dioxide we release (hence speaking to plants is good for them), but we all do this differently. Runners will develop high lung capacities to inhale and exhale large quantities of air. This can be measured in various ways but perhaps the most common is known as 'vo_2 max' or 'maximal oxygen consumption' (where v stands for volume, o_2 for oxygen). The average for men and women is between 27–40 millilitres of oxygen per kilogram of body weight, per minute. The capacity of athletes like Usain Bolt is recorded to be somewhere between 80 and 90 ml per kilo per minute. If we then remember that oxygen makes up 20 per cent of the air, then we are talking about a lot of air moving through a person's lungs in a minute. And bearing in mind that for a sprinter like Bolt, during the 10 seconds he takes to cover 100 metres, his feet are only touching the ground for 0.8 seconds of it. He is, practically speaking, almost airborne. While we are considering what are pretty superhuman athletes at their maximum efficiency, this is still extraordinary. Even for the average person, the estimates of how much air we actually breathe in a lifetime ranges from about 265 million litres upwards. That is a great deal of air.

This process of respiration is something that many organisms on the planet, not just humans, require to survive. All mammals are air breathers; even those that live in the seas must come to the surface to inhale and exhale air. Insects breathe but they do so differently. Rather than having fleshy lung sacks, insects inhale air through their exoskeletons by means of structures called 'spiracles' that open and close in order to deliver air to their trachea, almost directly into the bloodstream. What all of this respiration of air achieves is that which much of organic life requires to carry on living, for its cells to continue going and building and reproducing. At the heart of the work of our cells is a process known as 'cellular respiration' or 'aerobic respiration', the process by which the gases in the air – namely, oxygen – are effectively harnessed by a kind of combustion. Cellular respiration is essentially a chemical reaction that creates the energy that the cells need. Plants, of course, do this by photosynthesis, respirating air in a rather different way to animals.

Take stock of how all of this use of air – that is, all this life that depends on air – puts a considerable demand on it. Even though very recent inventions may suggest that human life may soon not be as reliant on the air as we have been used to, as scientists have devised ways to administer oxygen to air-deprived subjects by the injection of 'microparticles' of oxygen directly to the bloodstream, we should conclude that the air has a very important role to play indeed.

This book looks at air as not only a remarkable substance, intriguing natural phenomena or technological achievement, but something that surrounds and sustains us. It examines why air is so important; how we even came to know that air was there; and what it does, or is doing. It draws out how the air has shown itself, and how we first found it by harnessing and exploiting it. It is about air and how we have come to know it, feel it, sense it, but it is also about who we are and how we live with the air – our ways of life, our science, our culture, our politics, our technologies. The stuff of poetry, painting, literature and scientific inquiry, air gives sustenance to our imagination. Air, then, is not just of the world 'out there'; rather, it shapes all manner of expression and forms of representation – our stories, histories, thoughts, feelings and emotions are guided by it and may well be characterized by it. For the remainder of this Introduction I aim to trace a path through how we have come to know the air, first as a key substance of our planet's primeval development, then as an element of the ancient world, the object of Enlightenment science and invention and, finally, as a primary material in industrial, social and technological revolutions.

The birth of air

Where has our air come from and how has it altered? Today our atmosphere is made up of a common range of gases such as methane, ammonia, volatile amines, organic acids, hydrogen sulphide, nitrogen, nitrous oxide and more. But it was not always this way. Why is this? Our early atmosphere is thought to have been made up of predominantly hydrogen and helium, some of which were lost to space. Later, as the planet's gravity and magnetic fields became stronger, heavier gases were retained. High levels of volcanic activity meant that a significant proportion of carbon dioxide, methane and hydrochloric acid were added to the mix in what is called 'outgassing'. Much of the carbon dioxide during this period would begin to be locked into carbonate rocks and dissolved into the oceans that formed from cooling water vapour. And yet, perhaps the biggest thing to happen to our air was life.

Around 3.5 billion years ago, when organic bacteria and early organic forms first began on this planet, the atmosphere did not remain unchanged. What is notable about this time is that oxygen – that thing we require so much – did not exist in the air but was put there. Organisms began to regulate the circulations and cycles of gases in a way that began to oxygenate the air and thus provide more suitable conditions for aerobic life forms – life that depends on respiration. This kind of reciprocal air–earth relationship was not really a new hypothesis. Earlier 'exhalation' theories, espoused by the English naturalist John Woodward in the late seventeenth century, identified localized atmospheric events within geological origins, with meteorology being understood as an extension of geology and the depths of the planet. Modern meteorology would make far more convincing assertions that posited a cycle of interchanges and exchanges of matter and energy between the atmosphere, the earth and the seas.[1] But on a global level nobody had really understood how the emergence of our planet's atmosphere interacted with life, the seas and the earth's geology. This relationship, between organic life and the levels of gases such as oxygen, nitrogen and carbon dioxide in the air, was first posited as an answer in the 1970s by James Lovelock and Lynn Margulis, with their Gaia hypothesis. Such a rebalancing of the atmosphere helped to create the conditions that would maintain a higher oxygen-rich atmosphere and a relatively continuous temperature. For Lovelock, air thus functions as if it were a 'thermostat' on a central heating system, the atmosphere protecting life on the planet from potentially harmful or adverse changes.[2]

Lovelock's work would turn the heads of many scientists, not least because his hypothesis gave some kind of purpose to the biosphere and the atmosphere. Despite those problems, it importantly brought the atmosphere's emergence into a far greater relationship with life than was first thought. Lovelock would compare the atmosphere to a snail's shell or a mammal's fur. It also drew attention away from the earth, to outer space. His approach would prove valuable for examining the possible existence of life on other worlds because planetary atmospheres could be used to help predict the presence or absence of life. A particular climate would indicate the symbiotic relationship between the air and organic life forms interacting with it – the appearance of significant quantities of oxygen and methane together would be a primary marker. So what we find is that air stirs up some essential questions around life and the existence of it elsewhere.[3]

If the birth of air is tied up in the birth of life on earth, then that genesis is possible because air enables the transportation and distribution of material such as carbon into the sea or oxygen into the atmosphere. Despite its insubstantial appearance, over time the air can move vast quantities of materials. Let us explore briefly what is known as the Carboniferous age, a period several hundred million years ago, when the planet's huge stock-piles of carbon were made by the rapid growth of swamps and forests made up of bark-bearing trees, which eventually deposited thick sediments of coal. Caused by a so-called 'oxygen spike', the measurement of carbon isotopes in rocks and gas bubbles trapped in fossils otherwise known as 'fossil air' has seen the scientific community reach some accord. Although a more traditional approach would suggest that the climatic landscape of temperate swamplands and forests emerged from slow tectonic change, science has argued that it was the plants themselves that did it.

The massive oxygen spike (up to 35 per cent concentration of the atmosphere compared to its lower concentrations today) would lead to gigantism in amphibians and insects, especially huge dragonflies at over five times the length and twice the thoracic width of the largest existing dragonflies, with a reported 70-cm (28-in.) wingspan. But what caused the spike? According to several arguments, much of the world's bacteria and fungi that routinely broke down plant and vegetative matter had not yet evolved to break down a new molecule called 'lignin', a structural support that was enabling plants and trees to grow taller and with much thicker bark. The Carboniferous trees used lignin extensively and the inability of the bacteria to digest the trees – or rather their indigestion – led to the trees' carbon being buried underneath the swamps. It would not go back into the atmosphere but remained locked within the earth, lying in wait to be dug up during the Industrial Revolution as fuel. While it is not that easy to apply a correlation between higher oxygen levels and large mammal and insect development – as many insects did not achieve such gigantism – writing on 'Being the Right Size', the evolutionary biologist and socialist J.B.S Haldane (we will hear more about his father later) would suggest in 1928, 'If the insects had hit on a plan for driving air through their tissues instead of letting it soak in, they might well have become as large as lobsters.'[4] But it was not the insects driving oxygen through their tissues that made them larger but the higher oxygen levels. This allowed some insects to increase in size relative to their tracheal structure, which did not need to work so hard.

The point we need to return to is that the air and what was taken out of it and put back into it – namely, carbon by plant photosynthesis and oxygen by plant respiration – was incredibly important to the constitution of the atmosphere and, millions of years later, societies harnessing that carbon, and the cultural, political and scientific life that would evolve with it.

Ancient air

Some of the earliest philosophical inquiry of human civilization was concerned with how the air sat within a wider cosmology of other important elements. Even though these approaches strike a chord with the tumultuous earth we have just seen, this thinking sought to apply order and an elegance to the apparent chaos of a primeval world. During the revolution in scientific thinking in Ionia around sixth century BC, Presocratic thinkers such as

Anaximenes of Miletus, in contrast to later Platonic philosophy, saw spirit, soul and the air as one ambiguous element, a combination of the conception of the *pneuma* (spirit) and *aer* (material substance). Plato would later see air among four other primary elements in an arrangement we will come back to in a moment. For Anaximenes, however, the 'air is god'. In this thinking, air and breath are used synonymously. It is air in which we live, the air which holds us together and the air which is divine.

Even in these pre-modern registers of air there were profoundly modern efforts to try to sort air out. For instance, Aristotle would identify the air as the quality of 'passing-away', so that other elements could sometimes behave like air as they dissolved into the insubstantial. In some accounts, air was the primary element, as seen in Aniximenes' teacher Anaximander and his beliefs. Anaximander identified air as the essential and infinite element, the *aperion* from which water, earth and fire might be born. Air can become water when it is compressed. It becomes earth when cooled. And when rarefied and hot, it becomes fire. Thales, in contrast, saw the *aperion* as water, and Heraclitus as fire. Anaximenes sketched out a kind of hierarchy of elements, with air right at the top. Even the cosmos he considered to have been born from air. Whereas air for Homer was to be found somewhere more in the middle, between the earth and the copper canopy of the heavens; in Plato, air was alongside fire, water, earth and an intermediate aether that held them together.

Accounts of air have rarely remained consistent or uncontested. In spite of the theatrical and political mocking he would receive for his teachings, Aristotle would later reject this *aperion* too, aligning instead to Empedocles' four elemental 'bodies': earth, air, fire and water. These elements were yet laden with four specific combinable pairs of qualities – hot, dry, cold, moist – which could see each element combining or becoming another. Thus, air was hot and moist, fire hot and dry, water cold and moist and earth cold and dry. With these pairings we see an emergent classification of air brought into comparison with the other elements, which Plato would arrange into concentric rings around the centre of the universe.

Ancient mediations on the elements did not see air excluded to an ethereal and external realm independent of the human body, which was itself understood to be made up of compositions of elements as dispositions, or what the physician Hippocrates and much later, Galen (born AD 129), would divide into theories of the 'humours'. The Roman Galen would determine a world made of elements, seasons from years, and humans and their passions from humours. Yellow bile, blood, phlegm and black bile would give rise to four associated temperaments: sanguine, choleric, phlegmatic and melancholic. The humours were a balancing act, mixing and combining their temperaments with the elemental qualities of moist, cold, hot and dry, the body's internal circulations of blood, air, bile and phlegm, and the environmental climate. Galen would argue that it was in fact air, mixing with blood in the heart, that would ventilate and distribute warmth and vital spirit around the body, a thesis that William Harvey would later deny in his treatise on the body's circulation of blood in 1628 by asking, if 'fumes and air pass to and fro by this road . . . why can we find neither air nor fumes on dissection?' Preceded by Hippocrates' earlier treatise 'On Airs, Waters and Places', written around 400 BC, these approaches saw temperature mark temperament, unwholesome winds make behaviour, and races and nations made by the excitement of unpredictable and stormy weather.

In the majority of these pre-modern accounts, the air connects questions of the body to the workings of the cosmos and to the existence of a god and other deities. We need air for the essential order of things. We know air has particular qualities that bring it into play with other elements while it also distinguishes itself from them. Even more than that, air seems to be more, much more, than a simple material substance. A certain sort of vitality animates discussions and representations of air. Biblical accounts saw the air of a creator as the prime wind. In Genesis 2:7, for example, life is given through breath: 'And the Lord God formed man of the dust of the ground, and breathed into his nostrils the breath of life; and man became a living soul.' Meanwhile, Taoist world views have associated air with qi, and yogic traditions have

Prehistoric dragonfly
(*Meganeura manyi*).

15

seen it as a vital spirit which can be fostered through different breathing exercises.

On the weight of air

What tells us that the air is there? In part, this is a problem of effect. In other words, we know the air is there because of what it does. Figuring out what was *in* air would come down to a characteristically modern imperative to order and sort things beyond the four elements of the ancient world and various belief systems. In the 1650s Otto von Guericke from Saxony in eastern Germany probably invented the first modern air pump that could create a reasonable vacuum of air by pumping most of it away. His famous Magdeburg hemispheres were made of two halves of a copper sphere, around 50 cm (20 in.) in diameter and the joining edges were smeared with grease to create a seal. The air was sucked out using an airgun cylinder and a valve. At his famous demonstrations at the Reichstag in Regensburg in 1654, von Guericke showed that the vacuum had quite remarkable characteristics which would have not only scientific but theological implications. The problem was this: why was it that once the air was sucked out of the spheres it became extremely difficult to move the spheres apart?

Attaching two teams of sixteen horses on each side to attempt to pull the spheres apart, von Guericke showed that even the power of 32 horses could not cause the spheres to budge. Von Guericke argued that the horses were in fact attempting to pull against the 'mass of the air in the sky'. This was a theory of air pressure, the weight of the air that was pushing in at the spheres. In reality, von Guericke would need something more like 44 horses on either side to equal the 20,000 newtons, or 4,500 pounds force, pushing in at the spheres. But in demonstrating the properties of atmospheric pressure and by illustrating that the existence of a vacuum was even possible, something more was achieved. Von Guericke explicitly rejected the Aristotelian and Christian principle that a vacuum of air was an impossibility. Of course, von Guericke was likely building on

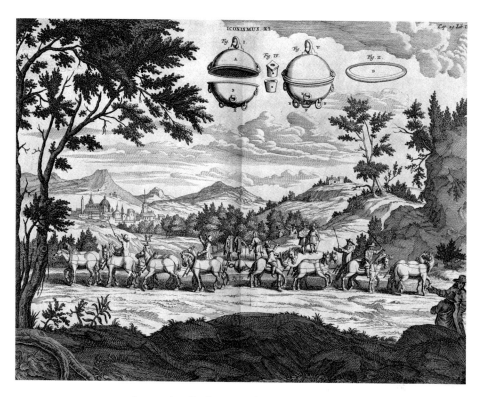

the work of others, such as the ingenious Hero of Alexandria, who had written his *Pneumatica* in the first century AD. Alongside other apparatus, Hero's 'Aeolipile' device illustrated the forces of heated, pressurized air exhausted as steam, which would cause an object to spin. Yet von Guericke was explicitly challenging accepted religious and scientific reason.

Von Guericke battled a philosophy which took a vacuum as nature's 'abhorrence'. Should something like air be removed from a space, then accordingly nature must infill that emptiness. This was why von Guericke's experiments created such discord and controversy. Indeed, it was so difficult to conceive that the air could not only exert such a powerful force, but that without air nothing could take its place. Von Guericke would publish his *Experimenta Nova* in 1672, setting out air as a physical substance and, in a chapter titled 'On the Weight of Air', its shape. He concluded that the pressure holding the spheres together was

17

Heron's Aeolipile, engraving from *Knight's American Mechanical Dictionary* (1876).

the weight of the atmosphere pressing down – a force that we would come to know as atmospheric pressure – all 15 lb per square inch of it, measured as a column of air from sea level to the top of the atmosphere.

Von Guericke's ideas would be developed by the Italian mathematician Evangelista Torricelli, known as the inventor in 1643 of one of the first barometers to measure atmospheric pressure. The Greek word *baros* of course means 'weight', here refering to the weight of the atmosphere – a position that had seemed unthinkable, given the apparent weightlessness of air. Almost simultaneously, the Englishman Robert Boyle took the production of a vacuum to new heights, publishing his *Touching the Spring of the Air, and its Effects* in 1660, which identified the air's 'restless endeavour to expand itself every way' and fill up small spaces. This was a quality of air that Boyle called its 'spring'. In Torricelli, importantly, we see the first technologies which illustrated that not only was air performing a force – pressure – but that the distribution of air was not the same everywhere in the world. It would be revealed how higher elevations, because of thinner air, would demonstrate diminishing pressure, as Pascal would, for his part, illustrate a few years after von Guericke at Puy-de-Dôme in the Auvergne, France. Von Guericke even noted that the diminished air pressure indicated that the space surrounding the Earth 'is not filled with air as far as the moon, much less the sun or beyond'.[5]

Sorting air out

Boyle's experiments and his air pump would be immortalized in Joseph Wright's *An Experiment on a Bird in the Air Pump* (1768). In the painting we see a bird choking, or crying out perhaps. Some of the spectators' faces look anguished. A child has her mouth open, resembling the bird's gasp; her eyes look right at it with concern. Some in the painting have turned away, immersed in their own lives or caught up in their own affairs. One spectator simply cannot watch. The image replicates those conducted by

Valentine Green after Joseph Wright, *An Experiment on a Bird in the Air Pump*, 1769, engraving.

scientists such as Boyle, who had placed a lark in a chamber to understand the effects of a vacuum on living organisms. At first, Boyle noticed that the bird began to droop, and then appeared sick, overtaken with convulsions. In Wright's image, air is what the contraption takes away, but life is sucked out too, and we feel it. In the image, we can almost see a tangible atmosphere that licks the room as if it has been pulled from the pump and is wafting its way round the spectators, who are dappled by the touch of the flickering candlelight emanating from the centre of the painting.

Wright's image anticipated his contemporary and fellow Lunar Society colleague, the theologian and natural philosopher Joseph Priestley (1733–1804). Priestley is widely attributed with the first discoveries of oxygen, or what he called 'dephlogisticated air', drawing on Georg Ernst Stahl's 'phlogiston' theory. Phlogiston was essentially an older alchemic presumption. It motivated the belief that to burn a substance, it must contain a component of fire, one of the ancient and essential primary elements. Should a material be burned, the decrease in its weight illustrated the

Ernest Board, *Joseph Priestley Hearing the News of the French Revolution*, 1912, oil on canvas.

loss of that phlogiston (or fire) to the air. Priestley took up this cause but advanced it further by coming to practically understand that air was an important part of a system.

It was on witnessing the expiration of small animals and organisms in a sealed container that Priestley decided in 1771 to see what would happen to a sprig of mint (really a small plant) in a glass jar. Somehow, the mint plant survived where other living organisms would not. The mint was doing something *to* the something that was in the glass jar. Priestley deduced that something had been restored by the mint which breathing and burning appeared to have exhausted, by phlogisticating the air to saturation point – the phlogiston he believed to have been released to the air from the candle or the body. The restored air could allow a candle to be burned in it, even though ten days earlier a flame had been extinguished in the same air. A small mouse would go on to survive for almost ten minutes. Priestley's later experiment in 1772 involved a mouse which lived for four-teen minutes without being hurt at all. Thus it allowed Priestley to notice air, and particularly what we now know were the properties of free oxygen, or O_2, in the interactions it had with animals, plants, lungs and people.

According to Priestley's physics, air was to be discovered 'in' things. It was taken from things, out of things. Rarely would he use the verbs 'compound', 'combine', 'decompose' or 'break down', which became the key verbs of modern chemistry. Instead, air was to be extracted or released. His first publication concerned a method of impregnating water with air, and even seeing plants photosynthesizing would not be understood as any kind of transformation or conversion. Instead, for Priestley, 'air exists in the green matter in a concentrated state from which light acts to disengage it'; it simply changes state.[6] In experimenting with water and plants and the purified air that the plants released, Priestley would argue that it was 'the Air contained in the water, and not the water itself that furnished the materials for this pure Air'.[7] Air was always present, it could just take a different form, or change its appearance. The air lost its 'aerial form' before retaining it in another context. But Priestley would lose his

Edouard Grimaux,
*Lavoisier Working with
His Wife the Chemist
Marie-Anne Pierrette
Paulze*, 1888,
heliogravure.

Lavoisier dans son laboratoire
Expériences sur la respiration de l'homme executant un travail
Fac-simile réduit d'un dessin de M...

argument to the French chemist Antoine Lavoisier (1743–1794), who is widely understood to be the father of modern chemistry. Indeed, what Priestley was calling 'dephlogisticated air' was not really the air itself, but the composition of oxygen molecules present in the air that was being aspirated by the mint plant and breathed in by the mouse.

Priestley was sorting out air to find it in things. But he was not really finding the elements that made up air, holding to a soon-to-be outdated theory of the elements that came from the Greeks. On the tails of Priestley's experiments and suspicious of phlogiston theory, in 1777 Lavoisier arranged an apparatus to heat mercury and air using a bell jar. The twelve-day experiment saw a red mercury oxide forming in the container and a drop in the volume of air. Indeed, he found that the air that was left could support no burning or life. He called this air *azote*, or 'no life', derived from the Greek for life, *zoe*. He would later term this 'azote nitrogen'. In collecting the oxide as powder and heating it, a colourless and odourless gas was produced that Lavoisier determined was oxygen, or Priestley's dephlogisticated air. After identifying these two separate gases, Lavoisier determined that the air was roughly made up of oxygen and nitrogen and in different proportions.

Following Priestley's work into modern chemistry helps us to identify how air began to be seen in terms of its qualities, its salubrity to breathe and, eventually via Lavoisier and others, the different substances that make up air. Advanced in Lavoisier's *Traité élémentaire de chimie* (Elemental Treatise of Chemistry), published in Paris in 1789, and like Priestley's careful use of test tubes and chambers to separate his different kinds of air, Lavoisier's modern chemistry broke down the elements into compounds and compositions, the basis for the periodic table. Air found itself decomposed and disaggregated into a remarkable table of simple substances, split thereafter into the gases oxygen, azote (nitrogen) and hydrogen (from which Lavoisier would later demonstrate was a part of water).

So we have determined by several seventeenth- and eighteenth-century experiments that air carries oxygen that allows organisms to breathe, while it can hold various other gases and substances. Air distributes a force we call 'atmospheric pressure'. Air made itself present in such a way that it demanded intense and exhaustive inquiry to discover what it was doing and how it worked. In the nineteenth century, John Tyndall would even discover that air had the ability to influence or 'scatter' light, which is why we see the sky as the particular colour blue, because

TABLE OF SIMPLE SUBSTANCES.

Lavoisier's 'Table of Simple Substances', 1789.

Simple fubftances belonging to all the kingdoms of nature, which may be confidered as the elements of bodies.

New Names.		Correfpondent old Names.
Light	- - -	Light.
Caloric	- - -	{ Heat. Principle or element of heat. Fire. Igneous fluid. Matter of fire and of heat.
Oxygen	- - -	{ Dephlogifticated air. Empyreal air. Vital air, or Bafe of vital air.
Azote	- - -	{ Phlogifticated air or gas. Mephitis, or its bafe.
Hydrogen	- -	{ Inflammable air or gas, or the bafe of inflammable air.

it has altered the wavelength of the light passing through it. Perhaps we can then say that these discoveries, particularly Priestley's and Lavoisier's discovery of oxygen, would not even have been possible were it not for air's peculiar ability to do so many things. The one thing we have seen most consistently is its capacity to distribute.[8] Scientific networks were irrefutably important in Priestley's discovery, his debate with Lavoisier, and the dissemination of his ideas through the coffee houses and scientific spaces of the eighteenth century, especially learned societies and groups of colleagues such as the Lunar Society, based in Derby. This included figures including Erasmus Darwin, Josiah Wedgwood, Matthew Boulton and James Watt, who would dramatically shape Britain's industrial and economic fortunes, as well as its scientific progress.[9] Air needed to be talked about.[10]

In other words, there was simply no 'I' in air's invention: scientific ideas developed in collaboration and dialogue. The question of air was 'in the air', so to speak. Furthermore, the ability for air to transport, communicate and deposit things underpinned the very discovery of itself. It was air's distribution of resources – especially carbon – that enabled our eighteenth-century scientists to investigate it. All the energy that was

James Sayers, *The Repeal of the Test Act: A Vision*, 1790, etching.

fuelling the Industrial Revolution and Priestley's research had come from the massive carbon deposits and the explosion of oxygen over 300 million years ago, as carbon was taken out of the air and put back into the ground through plant photosynthesis, bacterial indigestion and oxygen-driven animal and insect gigantism. The rich coal resources that made Priestley's work possible were right under his feet.

Revolutions of air

Earth, air, fire, water. Despite the separation of air into its constituent parts and the strong move away from these simple primordial building blocks, the following centuries saw air brought back into a turbulent relation with them. In the elemental pandemonium of mechanized industry and the subsequent growth of cities, air was harnessed with combustion, socioeconomic reorganization and unrest. In northern Europe, cities were the demonic places of mills, blast furnaces, chimneys belching out smoke – infernal places alluding to Milton's *Paradise Lost*. The violence of eighteenth-century change was essentially founded on the meeting of elements that threatened to build up to a revolutionary head of steam. The carbon deposits that enabled the wealth of Priestley's benefactors met with fire fed by the oxygen in the air to heat water into steam, a wet and pressurized air that in 1764 would drive the machine by the Scottish inventor James Watt to give efficient motive power to mechanize human movements. Watt's variation on the Newcomen steam engine drew on some of the properties of air we have been considering – notably, air pressure. The original engine utilized a condensing cylinder, with one end open to the atmosphere; the other part of the cylinder was found below a piston that drove a beam, which worked a mechanical pump. Steam was released into the cylinder, pushing the piston upwards. Cold water was then pumped into the cylinder, which cooled the steam back into water below the piston. This process created a partial vacuum, which saw the atmospheric pressure pushing the piston downwards, driving

Samuel Collings,
The Reverend Philosopher
(also known as *Dr
Phlostigon, the Priestley
Politician or the Political
Priest!*), colour trans-
parency, 1794, etching
and engraving.

the pump's alternate stroke. Watt's considerable improvement
on this design meant that the engine could run much more
efficiently and work in reverse, substantially widening its use.

This volatility of air combusting with water and earth
(coal) and fire would find its expression in political movements

– 'letting off steam', as it were – as if society were becoming a pressurized battle of people, machines and their masters. It is not incongruent then that Priestley's support for the revolution in France should see atmospheric analogies become vehicles for making sense of political turmoil. Jean-Pierre Houël's painting *Storming of the Bastille* visualizes the fortress ablaze during the events of 14 July 1789. Now picture Watt's engine of pressurized steam and condensing water. Smoke thrives in a tempest of air that threatens to engulf the fortress, but it is not clear where the thick smoke is coming from. Is it the fire inside the Bastille or the raging clouds above? The French historian Jules Michelet described the moments before the capture of the fortress in his distinctive historical semi-fiction. It was an evening that 'had been stormy, agitated by a whirlwind of ungovernable frenzy. With daylight, one idea dawned upon Paris.'[11] This was revolution, and the air was bubbling, ignited. Something had 'impregnated the air, the temperature has changed; it seems as though a breath of life has been wafted over the world'.[12]

James Scott after James Lander, *James Watt and his Steam Engine*, 1860, engraving on paper.

Jean-Pierre Houël,
Storm(ing) of the Bastille,
1789, watercolour.

In *A Tale of Two Cities* (1859), Charles Dickens reconstructs a similar scene. A tempestuous air describes the movement of the revolutionary crowd.[13] The noise is immense, gathering, 'like the growling of distant thunder, resounds nearer and nearer, rushing on with the rapidity and roaring of a tempest. The Bastille is taken.'[14] The revolution is a dangerous mixture of air and water, moving together as one. The sound of the crowd is all the breath of France, while their movement is a living sea; 'through the fire and through the smoke – in the fire and in the smoke', movements, materials and air multiply. Dickens repeats himself, over and over; 'muskets, fire and smoke', 'cannon, muskets, fire and smoke', 'cannon muskets, fire and smoke', slight displacements of the raging sea, 'blazing torches', 'shrieks', 'volleys', a boiling tumult that bursts and spits, leaping 'into the air like spray'.

Inspired by the events leading up to the French Revolution, Priestley was often caricatured spreading incendiary and insurrectionary smoke and hot air against the monarchy, religious intolerance and the 'landed classes'. Neither could he contain his enthusiasm for the events in Paris which he would characterize as like a freshening air, 'so favourable a wind', that would let 'every young mind expand itself, catch the rising gale, and partake of the glorious enthusiasm'.[15]

The razing of Priestley's house in the Birmingham riots of 1791 is clearly not a million miles away from Houël's Bastille depiction. A mob had formed against Priestley and other dissenters who were meeting at Dadley's Hotel in Temple Row in the centre of Birmingham to celebrate the Bastille Day anniversary. The mob gathered outside and shouted 'Church and King forever!' before burning down the new meeting house where Priestley was minister. They then headed over to Priestley's house at Fairhill, which they razed to the ground before smashing his laboratories.[16] Priestley would escape to America in April 1794 aboard the *Sansom*, anchoring first in Sandy Hook before navigating New York Harbor. He would go

The Reverend Dr Priestley's House at Fairhill following the Birmingham Riots, 1792, coloured aquatint.

with many messages of luck. One was from the Society of United Irishmen of Dublin, who made a vague comparison between Priestley and gunpowder. His was a force that 'might impel the air, so as to shake down the strongest towers and scatter destruction'. Lavoisier, Priestley's great rival and an aristocrat, did not fare so well. He was executed a month later on 8 May during the Robespierre Terror.

Steam demon

The turbulent conditions in France by the mid-nineteenth century would be compared to the rapidly evolving unfamiliar air of industrial innovation produced since Watt's invention; a force described as a 'Proteus Steamdemon' in Thomas Carlyle's characterization of the cotton mill in the 1840s. The engine seems to make the world boil and simmer with fumes, all life is a bewilderment. With Henry Mayhew's balloon ascent over London on 13 September 1852, he found it impossible to distinguish the monstrous form of the city from Hell or the heavens. Yet his view on to London would have been quite different to the one the balloonist Vincenzo Lunardi had seen 68 years previously in 1784. While Lunardi delighted in the inexpressible and calming atmosphere of the balloon and saw his earthly worries depart, Mayhew was grateful to be up and apart from London's demonic air. Taking a breather, Mayhew's is an 'angel's view' from up the 'aerial ladder'; he is safe from the city:

> where, perhaps, there is more virtue and more iniquity, more wealth and more want, brought together into one dense focus than in any other part of the earth – to hear the hubbub of the restless sea of life and emotion below, and hear it, like the ocean in a shell, whispering of the incessant strugglings and chafings of the distant tide and feel, for once, tranquil as a babe in a cot, and that you are hardly of the earth, earthy, as, Jacob-like, you mount the aerial ladder, and half lose sight of the 'great commercial world' beneath, where men are regarded as mere counters to play with, and where

to do your neighbour as your neighbour would do you con-
stitutes the first principle in the religion of trade – to feel
yourself floating through the endless realms of space, and
drinking in the pure thin air of the skies.[17]

A balloon prospect
over London, 1880,
lithograph.

A few years later, Marx's 'Speech at the Anniversary of the
People's Paper' (in 1856) elicited a different view on the 'strug-
glings and chafings'. Marx's perspective is definitely not
Mayhew's. He is not from above but from within – inside the
atmospheres of London. He describes a climate produced by the
principal agent of industrial change again: the steam engine. The
societal transformations of steam, for Marx, made possible an
oppressive air of inequity that became so heavy it weighed in on
one as almost an atmospheric pressure, pushing downward 'with
a 20,000 lb force'. 'Do you feel it?' he would ask.[18] It was the hot
and accelerated air of steam that was powering a revolution in
labour practices and manufacturing, as well as the tawdry
working and living conditions of the working classes that Marx
and Engels wanted to expose.[19] Marx sought to awaken the
public to their immersion in the atmosphere and their class

struggle, to feel the inequality Mayhew delights in being able to escape, if only for a moment.

While Marx demanded that the pressures of political and social upheaval be noticed, the new airs of modernity distracted many from them or encouraged them to seek escape in other forms. In Walter Benjamin's scattered remarks in his unfinished *Arcades Project*, a small vignette of the pre-Surrealist Grandville and his *Another World* (1844) takes shape, in an excerpt which features a fantastical little hobgoblin who is trying to find his way around outer space. What he finds or constructs is a bridge made of iron. The piers rest on planets, the bridge between them forming a 'causeway of wonderfully smooth asphalt', and as the causeway reaches Saturn, the rings appear as a circular balcony on which the inhabitants of Saturn stroll to take in the fresh air. Grandville's iron bridges find their mirror in the Paris Arcades beloved of Benjamin's strolling *flâneurs*, interior kaleidoscopes of colour and consumption sculpted by iron and glass. The airs of Grandville's hobgoblin are those of an escapist, evacuating from toil to a place of leisure and contemplative oneiric dreaming. His works were appreciated by Baudelaire, and are full of subversive and anthropomorphized subjects often made of, surrounded by, cloaked within, or seen to be exhausting, air.

This dreamscape of smoking sketch pens, steaming harps, flying bellows and other aerial things was possibly a nostalgic one. With the fall of Napoleon Bonaparte and the restoration of France's monarchy there resulted for Benjamin a 'suffocating world' of pomp that would mark the end of the Arcade, where

> Every stone bears the mark of despotic power, and all the ostentation makes the atmosphere, in the literal sense of the words, heavy and close . . . One grows dizzy with this novel display; one chokes and anxiously gasps for breath.[20]

The iron in Grandville's pre-Surrealism was notably light, organizing an interplanetary, peripatetic gaze of a modernity marked more by revolutions in speed and motion than stability.

This fleetingness was captured in the canvases of Impressionism, for as the steam engine sped up production and urban life, it accelerated experiences of time and space. In rocketing its way through the air and across the landscape, new and amazing forms of visual representation, writing and poetry were born with the train; each image and word seeking to convey a sense of speed and dynamism, as though forms melting into thin air. Take J.M.W. Turner's *Rain, Steam and Speed* (1844), for example. Although initially disparaged, Turner's painting has become an icon of modern mobility. The railway fired by coal and steam blasting its way through the landscape, proclaims, for Michael Adas, a machine that challenges 'the elements themselves'.[21] The railway seemed to turn everything to air. Speed out-natures nature; the image is a dissolution of anything fixed. Everything is vaporized into the burning of air, light, rain and landscape.[22] What we see in Turner's painting is that modern air is light. And as with the arcades, the air of somewhere, even a building such as the Crystal Palace in London, was incandescent. For Marshall Berman's exploration of Dostoevsky's meditation *Notes From Underground* (1864), the weightlessness of the iron and glass building is comparable to Turner's painting. The Crystal Palace was designed by Joseph Paxton for the Great Exhibition of 1851, and it seemed that Paxton was a master of air. Even as the head gardener at the

J.J. Grandville, illustration from *Un Autre Monde* (1844).

stately home Chatsworth House in Derbyshire, he preceded the Crystal Palace with the great conservatory and other warmed-glass structures. With boilers and extensive pipework, ventilators in the brickwork and the roof, Paxton engineered temperate and subtropical climates to grow palms and lilies. The Palace's model was 84 m (277 ft) long, 37 m (123 ft) wide and 20 m (67 ft) high. Initially located in Hyde Park, once it was moved to Sydenham (a southeast London suburb), the Palace was lit up in a 'vividly chromatic and dynamic ambience'. Both painting and palace dazzled. Drenched with radiance, the spectator of both would appreciate the sun, sky and the water in the air shimmering together.[23]

J.M.W. Turner,
Rain, Steam and Speed:
The Great Western
Railway, 1844,
oil on canvas.

If steam was the engine of industry, leisure and faster forms of transport, the mobility it enabled would even alter the sensorium of war in a turbulent and romantic imagination of the Sublime. The air's association with revolution and violence saw accounts from some of the first war correspondents that were

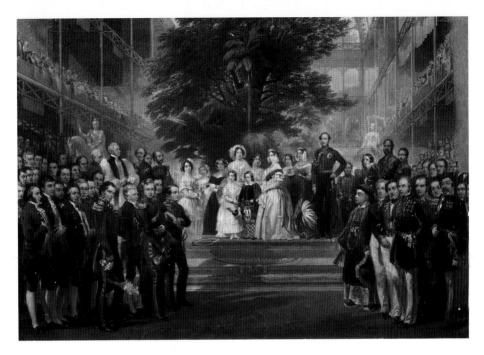

akin to Turner's paintings. Consider how William Howard Russell captures the steam-driven ships of the Anglo-French task force leaving the Crimea to capture the Russian base at Sebastopol in 1854:

Henry Courtney Selous, *The Opening of the Great Exhibition, 1st May 1851*, oil on canvas.

> The fleet, in five irregular and straggling lines, flanked by men-of-war and war steamers, advanced slowly, filling the atmosphere with innumerable columns of smoke, which gradually flattened out into streaks and joined the clouds . . . The land was lost to view very speedily beneath the coal clouds and the steam clouds of the fleet, and as we advanced, not an object was visible in the half of the great sky which lay before us, save the dark waves and the cold sky . . . Behind us was all life and power – vitality, force and motion.[24]

Ironically, it was then in fire and smoke that the Crystal Palace would alight for the last time when it burned to the ground in 1931.

External View of the Transept of the Crystal Palace from the Prince of Wales Gate, 1851, coloured lithograph.

Before present

If we can reconcile air as an important conveyor of things, we can also assume that it has gone through an awful lot of transformations and changes, possibly irreversibly. At the turn of the twentieth century other advances were taking place in radioactivity and the discovery of new elements whose qualities were rather ethereal. Radium gave off light, it made impressions on photographic plates, it gave out heat, it emanated into the air and it even enabled an electric current to be passed through the air that surrounded it. For Marie Curie, whose work to isolate and understand it proved Nobel Prize-winning, radium was 'contagious'. Like an airborne disease, it took to the atmosphere readily. 'Dust', she wrote, 'the air of the room . . . The air in the room is a conductor', and little could be protected from it, should it not contaminate all other objects and apparatus with its radioactivity.

By 1950 the u.s. Atomic Energy Commission (AEC) was responding to the numerous concerns of scientists and advocates on the potential effects of nuclear testing on the atmosphere. The radiative properties of strontium-90 and plutonium – the two main cancerous and toxic isotopes of concern – gave particular

shape to the debate. Strontium 90, a manmade element, is now present in practically every single life form that exists on the surface of the planet because its isotopes have been suspended in the atmosphere by the tests, coming slowly to rest on bodies, islands, landscapes and cities in the years that followed.

What distinguishes the radiating properties of atmospheric suspension from others is their apparent lack of a centre – they

The Baker Nuclear Explosion of Operation Crossroads, 1946.

do not seem containable to any one place. Air, in this sense, becomes both personal *and* planetary, it is complex, uncertain and nonlinear, a fallout turning the atmosphere into a weapon. Air is but the transporting mechanism to deliver radiation thousands of miles away. Nuclear testing in the Pacific islands of Micronesia in 1952 subjected those far-off places to a visual and climatological scrutiny.[25] The Bikini Atoll 'cauliflower' and

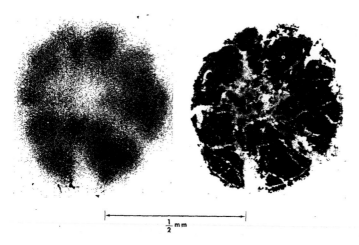

C. Adams, J. D. Connor, 'Thin Section and Radioautograph of a Fallout Particle', 1957.

'mushroom' clouds of atom bombs detonated beneath the waves and above them became the most photographed events on the planet.

The subsequent political and radioactive fallout from the tests would help to disturb some kind of 'nuclear uncanny', a sensory disorientation produced by or through the action of radiation which would connect islands, cells and the globe because of the air. The air was transporting radioactive effects inside the boundaries and barriers of the atmosphere to the skin, suturing the body with the atmosphere for ever. Through air and radiation, the nuclear fallout penetrated as an invisible force, tending to concentrate in particular areas of the body irradiating the surrounding tissues. Leading to cancers and leukaemia, it was as if the radioactive air created little bubbles of too-virile life inside the body.

The air's nuclear contamination seems to work from the inside out. A weird fear from everywhere, the atmosphere of the mid-twentieth century was marked by looming bombers, instantaneous vaporization, cancers and the fallout of materials that would take years to settle to the ground. In this elliptical or non-linear kind of worry, it is appropriate that it was the uncanny and radioactive properties of nuclear testing that enabled the scientist Willard Libby to develop one of the most precise forms of dating we have. In 1960 Libby won the Nobel Peace Prize for his work for

Tess Hurrell, *Chaology No 1.*, 2006, gelatin silver print.

effectively inventing carbon dating, a process developed at the University of Chicago Institute for Nuclear Studies, which was also heavily involved in the development of the understanding of the atmospheric effects of nuclear weapons. His work included the fallout from high-atmosphere explosions that had been seen in the United States and in tests conducted by France, Britain and Russia.[26] Working on the principle that carbon-14 has a half-life of 5,600 years, his methods would suppose that a body 5,600 years old would be half as radioactive as an organism living today.[27] Quaternary science and archaeology soon started to refer to 1950 as the present, not because of the emergence of Libby's groundbreaking techniques, but because attempting to use radiocarbon dating from beyond that point proved very difficult. The sharp spike in carbon-14's presence in the atmosphere from the nuclear bomb tests meant that dating after 1950 was unreliable. In archaeological and Quaternary science, carbon dating would provide a new measure of the present. Rather than use the old Christian calendar of BC and AD, Libby's work led the way for BP, or 'before present'. So while the explosions would be archived in photographs, the atmosphere and our bodies, Tess Hurrell's work committed them to sculpture using cotton wool, talcum power, wire and pipe-cleaners.

The infinitude we see in air makes the atmosphere loom so large that it seems beyond us, surpassing the smaller-scale changes commentators were already beginning to notice in the foul air of the eighteenth- and nineteenth-century metropolis, something that we will explore later. In both senses, argues the cultural historian Steven Connor, 'it is immense, and it is waste ... a nothing, an out of sight and out of mind'.[28] The air is paradoxically an easy thing to forget or ignore. On the other hand, the air is dependent on the life it makes possible. And the fact that we have not seemed to mind using it, dirtying it, exhausting it, wasting it, at least until quite recently in our history, means that it is possible to track quite significant shifts and changes in the proportions of a gas like carbon dioxide in our air, now found in quantities of almost 400 parts per million in 2012, compared with closer to 280 ppm in 1860. This has led many physical and natural scientists to refer to our current geological epoch as the 'Anthropocene' (*anthropos* meaning 'man', and *ceno*, 'new').

The following chapters follow these themes to explore the discovery, exploration, manipulation and expression of air in a variety of different contexts, times and places. They reflect air's liveliness and volatility, its refusal to stay in one place and to confound. They explore how air has sustained perplexing scientific questions; how it helps us to make sense of tumultuous social and economic conditions; and how it even tells us about death, providing us with the poetic vocabulary to express the movements of the passions. Air is not only chemically made up but it makes us up, moving things and us. Air shapes our lives and the way we live and make sense of them.

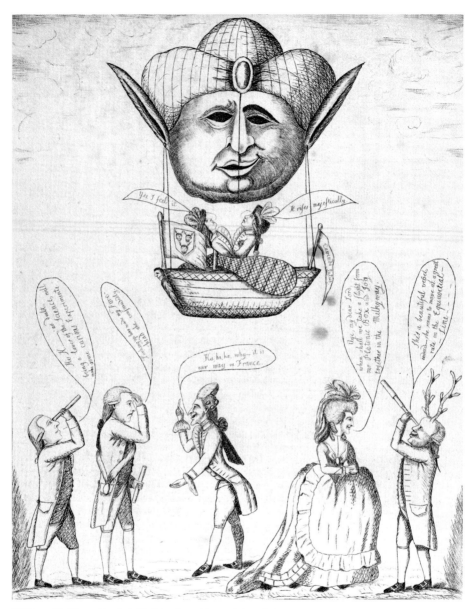

W. Dent, *The Devonshire Aerial Yacht*, 1784, etching and drypoint.

1 Airborne

It seems we have taken to the air.[1]

On 26 October 1929, a baby girl was born in an aeroplane flying above Miami, Florida. The birth was not an accident. Dr Thomas W. Evans and his wife Margaret D. Evans had chartered a Fokker Trimotor with the intent of delivering the first air-born baby. Departing from the one-year-old Pan American Field (now Miami International Airport), doctors, nurses, a co-pilot and the baby's maternal grandmother were all on board the plane. The aircraft circled the Dade County Courthouse at 1,200 feet during the birth, which occurred twenty minutes after takeoff. The plane then flew over Biscayne Bay for several minutes before landing. Mother and baby were transported to the hospital. The baby girl was not named 'Airogene', 'Biscayne', 'Pan Skymiss', 'Skylove', or the many other names suggested to parents by well-wishers. Instead they chose 'Airlene'.[2]

Air, writes philosopher Luce Irigaray, is something we are born into even if we are not on board an aeroplane above Miami, as Airlene indeed was.[3] Birth marks our first sound – the baby's cry – which of course is a gasp for air, for life. But in that moment the environment is no longer outside us. We come out into the air, reaching for it and bring it inside. In a way, we become air-born(e) as soon as we leave the womb.

The first successful efforts to get people aloft by powered flight played on the idea that being born to the air came with a similar gasp. This was both a rallying cry and perhaps restoration of some sort of break or disconnection with the ground. These moments of ascension were cast as more metaphorical births than Airlene's literal delivery. Baptized by social and spiritual uplift, to live and move in the air would create a new and improved sort of human, modern aerial-citizens of the future who would live out the promise of the air.

Curiously, the balloon never quite achieved the same kinds of expression, never reaching the same and simultaneous spiritual and secular adoration, even if it did achieve a certain sort of mania much earlier in Britain and France. By the late 1700s, balloon mania hit home in Europe, the early flights by Lunardi and Jean-Pierre Blanchard were a strange mix of scientific experimentation and fervent popular spectacle. Balloons could carry instruments to measure layers in the atmosphere, the formation of weather, the electrical charges within clouds, identifying and measuring pressure and temperature. Blanchard was helped by Dr John Jeffries in these experiments, but also in public support by Georgiana Cavendish, Duchess of Devonshire, who was keen to align herself and the Whigs to the balloon cause. Georgiana sponsored Blanchard's flight in 1794 – the year Priestley left Britain for America – from Grosvenor Square in London. The balloon, nicknamed the 'Devonshire Aerial Yacht', quickly succumbed to derision and caricature.

This was not the first or last time that Georgiana would be associated or portrayed with, or of, air. In the same year, Sir Joshua Reynolds's painting of the duchess saw the form of her portraiture born out of fog. While in 1783, Maria Cosway would paint Georgiana as Cynthia from Spenser's *The Faerie Queen*. But she might also resemble the goddess Diana, commanding the clouds and the heavens. As the Roman goddess, Georgiana becomes Diana's derivative, *dium* and *dius*, or sky and light.

So the balloon flirted with the new atmospheric sciences and a sometimes more cynical kind of passion for all things rising. Moreover, the balloon was a fairly good metaphor for whimsy. Balloons featured in many late eighteenth-century satirical prints as if to frame anything that needed 'sending up' with humour or ridicule – to quickly deflate egos with the flatulent, superfluous air of the balloon.

Valentine Green after Maria Cosway, *Portrait as Cynthia from Spenser's 'The Faerie Queen'*, 1783, engraving.

The aeroplane could take the idea of inhabiting air to another level of interest. From Soviet Russia we see Stalin holding a child in his arms, a woman breastfeeding an infant, and – in-between – three aircraft swooping from the sky. The representation is about the national community.[4] It is a relation suckled by motherland, sky and the Father, Stalin, for the 'life and health of every child'.[5] You might see the halo circling Stalin and the child (halos again), and the aircraft, as flying from or descending perhaps from the heavens, and the breastfeeding woman as a reference to the mother or Madonna, nourishing the nation. Although in Russia the air and the plane were mobilized as a way to replace and separate the Church from State, the aeroplane's birth in Russia could not help but reproduce the spiritual overtones of ascensional conversion. One's first flight was sometimes called a 'baptism', a rebirth from the ground to the air.

A new encounter of spiritual transcendence was being performed in the cathedral of the sky. Flight became ritual. In Soviet Russia, it was the party and the leader, not the Orthodox Church

Paul Sandby, *Coelum ipsum petimus Stultitia,* 1784, etching and aquatint.

that were to be the spiritual family of the nation. 'Aerial baptisms' were performed in the countryside by Soviet aviators, bringing the people out of their supposed lethargy, ignorance and poverty. The aviators would deliver speeches on the benefits of aviation, give out literature and information and, critically, bring local people on board for a tour of the aeroplane and the air. These were conversions, a metamorphosis by air, not water. The air baptism (*vozdushnoe kreshchenie*) could immerse the peasant in a rational and scientific space of technology, to let them see that 'there was no God, angels, or other celestial spirits in the heavens'.[6] The once 'isolated' and 'unwashed' would be 'choked with happiness' on their return to the ground, sharing the exhilaration of a secular awakening.

In the United States aviation was quite different. Flight was the umbilical link to what Robert Corn termed the 'Winged Gospel', an association of flying with spiritual matters in an Evangelical Christian tradition.[7] Everything, it seemed, was destined for the air, from radio to skyscrapers. And in that medium they would find a new kind of enthusiasm, a 'free-for-all of spiritual energy'.[8] To fly was to become divine, the massive transportation of society 'to the heavens'. But like the Gospel, flight needed to be spread and urged. America had to become awakened and flyers such as Lindbergh symbolized this view. Lindbergh was dashing, heroic and angelic in his movement, landing at Le Bourget airfield near Paris on 21 May 1927. Lindbergh, the 'Galahad of the Air', emanated a calm self-confidence, an aura of reserves yet to be tapped. Ultimately, figures and heroes like Lindbergh became models on which the new air-minded aerial subject would be compared and fashioned.

The United States was probably the most ardent advocate of air-mindedness. For the young and by the young, air-mindedness was even bound up in other aerial technological initiatives that harnessed the ethereal world of radio waves to promulgate the Gospel. Debates were broadcast on the four main radio networks in a series of events titled the *Convention of the Air*. One of the most interesting took forward an earlier idea coined by Robert H. Hinckley, Assistant Secretary of State for Commerce, who had borrowed the phrase 'air conditioning'. Hinckley had wanted to promote the 'infiltration' of aerial practice and knowledge about flight, and like Priestley, Hinckley saw that air could be pushed into things. The air could take form in another subject and even a syllabus of education. Hinckley was already heavily influential in the inception of the Civilian Pilot Training Program – America's massive pilot recruitment scheme that had begun in 1938, and the promotion of all things aeronautic within the social sciences. Hinckley would even go on to co-found the US ABC radio network in 1946, which saw flight mix with radio and other forms of cultural expression, especially jazz. Multiplying the mood, feeling and rhythm of the religious fervour, jazz arrived airborne just at the right time as 'planes toured the heavens, and buildings competed with clouds'.[9]

N. L. Engelhardt, Associate Superintendent of Schools in New York, was the author of a speech that took up Hinckley's challenge. America's educators would have to surpass the contented 'use of the air', he argued, 'for breathing alone'.[10] The world, its sciences, peoples and politics, were told in a new aerial syntax. Junior students could learn about birds and seeds, while those in junior high would contemplate the idea of living *in* the *air* instead of *on* the *earth*. They should 'breathe deeply for health's sake'. Theirs was a new climate of education.

Aerodynamic

Before Lindbergh and his contemporaries was the French scientist and chronophotographer Étienne-Jules Marey who is well known for his breakthroughs in time-motion studies with other luminaries such as Eadweard Muybridge, Frederick Taylor and John and Lillian Gilbreth. Marey was hard at work studying the motions of birds and insects in the late 1880s. His research abstracted movement into an essence of pure physical motion. In this space, motion was diagnosed, copied, improved and imposed. By exploring what gave animals flight, Marey could reproduce that motion within a model or simulation of an insect. Later he would recreate a bird and eventually build an aircraft.

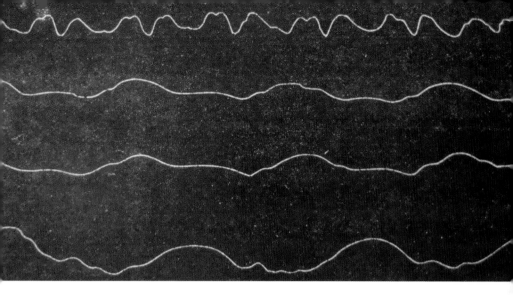

Étienne-Jules Marey, chronophotographic tracings of a duck, owl and a wild and common buzzard, 1874.

Employing time-motion photographic techniques for the analysis of birds in 1871 would not help Marey get much further in understanding the physiological attributes needed to generate flight. All his abstractions could do was to simply re-present flight into tiny movements. His new air pump-powered insect flight machine would change this. After numerous experiments on the insects he had reproduced in his model, he was able to establish the frequency at which the insects beat their wings – an incredible 390 times per second in a loop or figure-of-eight pattern.[11] The insect was not the only source of this complex motion. The insect's wings did not exert multiple or competing muscular groups, but rather just one movement of lowering the wing. Marey found that this muscle movement – accomplishing quite an elegant yet complex motion of the wing – had to be acted upon by another force. It was the resistance of the air which had caused the wing to deviate from its rectilinear movements of elevation and depression.[12] Marey's experiments on birds would consist of a procedure of tying the bird to an apparatus. At the other end of the apparatus was a mechanical bird, driven by the machine to emulate the motion of the real bird. By taking the trace of the movement of the bird's wings, the apparatus could be corrected until it precisely followed the movements of the real avian.

As air began to make itself known as resistance, Marey started to draw his work together from the aerodynamics and physiology of insects and birds to the visual abstractions of his chronophotography. The perfect aerial body would be a machine. But how to understand the relation to the air and its resistance? Marey went on from his mechanization of aerial animals and insects to the use of smoke. In employing all his ingenuity and knowledge to develop the first photographed aerodynamic tests that would allow him to capture in gorgeous aesthetic prints the motion of smoke around balloons, aeroplanes and other objects, air became visible. Accelerating air to understand the behaviour of objects in the air or in flight was, of course, not Marey's genius. Frank H. Wenham, a member of the Aeronautical Society of Great Britain, designed the first wind

NACA Wind tunnel in testing at Langley, Virginia.

The Transonic Wind
Tunnel at Langley.

tunnel in 1871 which used a steam-driven fan to propel air down
a tube to a model aircraft, effectively simulating the model's flight
and the effects of drag and lift. America's National Advisory
Committee for Aeronautics (NACA, later NASA), established in
1915, developed British ideas into many iterations of their
'atmospheric wind tunnel' at Langley Field Virginia in 1920.
Built to an ever-increasing scale, the tunnels would see the form
of aircraft shaped by the principles of moving air.

As the wind tunnel would evolve the understanding of aerodynamics and the development of the airfoil, what Marey
showed was even more aesthetic, revealing the motion of air
itself. Marey's air was forced into a stream of vapour, the stripes
across the black background like 'the strings of a lyre', or the
stretched 'strings like those of a piano'.[13] Always a contradiction,
even if his work would help to remove air's superfluous or ineffi-
cient eddies and currents, Marey's smoke tests produced some of
the most visually arresting and beautiful images.

The airborne body was required to adapt to these stream-lined models of motion. Like smoke passed through filters, it had to be efficient, physical, cerebral, entrained. Moreover, it was likely to be male. Abstract three-dimensional airspace was the ideal vantage point for masculine power to look over 'fertile female earth'.[14] Even female pilots were often characterized in terms of their unusual, abnormal manliness such as Pancho Barnes, the aviation legend.[15] Pilots were meant to be almost aerodynamic and athletic, youthful. With an 'aura of immortality' and impossibility, women pilots like Stella Wolfe Murray perpetuated the gospel myth. They were 'aerial missionaries', spreading the gospel of flight and the gospel 'by flight'.

Like America, Germany and Russia's experience was drawn from an agrarian and pastoral ideal. While America's towns and cities looked upon aviation as a form of civic boosterism, as would Russia, Germany's aviation movement shared considerable disdain for the cities, the swamp of Berlin and the materialism of modern life. The gliding movement was surely Germany's answer to America's gospel. Gliding was becoming widely 'regarded a patriotic declaration of faith'.[16] The discovery of thermals in the late 1920s meant a new imagination of the sky was suddenly etched with the topographies of mountainous chimneys – warm uplifting air that would thrust a glider higher. During weekends in the Rhön, thousands of the young would join glider clubs, taking part in singsongs around the fire. With their safe and calloused, hardworking aerial hands, the young gliders seemed to express Germany's self-confidence, a belief in the air and its future.

Crash, or fast air

Harvey Hanford has been framed. He was beaten up, cuffed and chained. In the silent Paramount Artcraft movie *The Grim Game* (1919), the young journalist Harvey Hanford escapes prison, a bear trap and the violence of his wife's captors. In the film's finale, Harvey and his wife race in a biplane just out of the reach of their chasers, an appropriate aerial escape – in contrast to the

Harry Houdini in
the *Grim Game*, 1919.

film's advertising posters, which showed numerous uniformed
service personnel and officials attempting to hold Harvey down.
Harvey hangs suspended on a rope between two biplanes. The
planes collide and one crashes to the ground. Only the collision
was real; the crash a fakery. The movie cuts together quite convin -
cingly the real collision of the planes, with a staged clip of a plane
hitting the ground headfirst in the midst of a small town. The
plane crumples on impact and turns upside down, before a dust
storm drifts out from beneath it to cloud the scene and envelop
the spectators. Harvey – as if a magician weaving his magic con-
cealed by the smoke – is then revealed to have survived. There is
considerable movie magic going on here, even in the film's late
scene. Harvey Hanford was played by Harry Houdini, and the film
was really a vehicle for his burgeoning celebrity status. While
Houdini's stunts and daredevilry were used heavily to promote the
film, so was the mid-air collision, with the publicity campaign
claiming that all the events were real.

Flight would elicit a new way to express our relation with air.
It could liquefy the solid footing of the ground, yet somehow
make the air that bit more tangible, that bit more 'there'.
Antoine de Saint-Exupéry describes the moment his character
Bernis starts his plane up in *Southern Mail*. The wind of the pro-
pellers makes the grass behind move 'like a stream', the ground

on takeoff stretches and distorts. The air 'at first impalpable, then fluid and now solid', the plane finds its footing and soars.[17] Everything becomes aqueous. Bernis is suspended, surfing the swells of air currents like a wave. He leans on the waves, bobs up and down on them as if in a boat and is ultimately swept away. The 'aspiration of air', or for air, is not about air's absence as if a vacuum. For the Italian Futurists, this meant evacuation and expurgation. Filippo Marinetti felt his chest 'open up like a great hole through which, smooth, fresh and torrential, all the blue of the sky plunged exquisitely', his earthbound passions and thoughts vomited forth.[18] Exorbitant, air is in the wrong place. Moving up to the air would be one form of escape to a better, cleaner, purer, accelerated air.

Being borne to the air in this way is not passive but deliberate. Advocates of the open-air movement in 1930s Britain would dart up hills, hike and navigate the countryside, as David Matless has explained.[19] Maybe wind could purify, shape and save the aerial-born before they even left the ground. Sefton Brancker, Director of Civil Aviation, would write a strange message in 1920 to recruits of the Royal Air Force College at Cranwell, Lincolnshire. In the college magazine, he spoke of a dream he once had of his 'aerial ancestors'. He had become a tribesman, who was trying to jump over a ravine when it appeared he would fall short. A gust of wind filled the man's cloak and carried him to safety. 'I rubbed my eyes. The cricket was still going on. The College was still behind me. I was still lying in the long grass. I got up, and started to walk to the Mess for tea.'[20] At Cranwell, the Lincolnshire landscape was the ideal location for this air-conditioned moulding of body and spirit for flight, evoking a preservationist return to a kind of England that once was.

At Cranwell, as aircraftman T. E. Shaw, T. E. Lawrence's Brough 'Bruff' motorbike saw him racing across Lincolnshire. On its straight roads and rolling countryside he and his bike flew, launching themselves like a projectile. The motion was all a whir. Wheels were sent 'into the air at the takeoff of each rise', the bike like the aircraft it copies.[21] Fused, Lawrence saw his bike as a 'logical extension of our faculties, and the hint, the provocation, to excess conferred by its honeyed untiring smoothness'. Lawrence challenges a Bristol fighter to a straight race back to the airfield. This is a race he apparently wins. Cranwell's climate is perfect, an ecosystem of airmindedness that can be found in its nooks and crannies and parade grounds. The hangar had its own 'private smell', the 'oil, acetone and hot metal', perhaps misunderstood by the outsider. In the sun, the hangar is ignited by light, whilst during a storm it comes alive as the doors tremble. Wind rattles through the hangar's many holes and imperfect surfaces, so that the structure becomes a kind of wood-wind-metal instrument, 'screaming on every high note of the scale, to raise devil-dances across the dusty floor. Screech, boom.'[22]

Lawrence sees evident difference between his instructors who come from an earlier age of soldiering. At first, Lawrence and his colleagues resist what he describes as the 'gas of militarism, which is breathed at us', but this resistance does not hold fast. The bulky Flight Commander Tim leads and inspires, he is a 'barometer' that sets 'the flight's weather' with the 'most exciting climate in the world'. At the flag-call, they cannot ignore the triumphalism and the rise to action held in the trumpet's cry. The sounds, Lawrence suggests, goes through them as an air

> however densely we close our pores. The thrill of
> exceeding sharpness conquers, in blades, sounds, tastes
> . . . Imagine a raw wind, and a wet early sunshine, making
> our shadows on the tarred ground the exact blue colour
> of our clothing.[23]

The recruits come to enjoy 'panting-out' their bodies in drill just for the fun of it, expelling the used air as if prophesying the future jet engine. Frank Whittle's invention is embodied in the recruit's gulps and exhaust(ion) of air. Everything is intense. They feel alive.

Up in the air

Accelerating through the air would fulfil the Futurists' desire for speed, wind and exhilaration. The flight that eventually killed Lawrence as he crashed from his motorbike was, of course, Marinetti's impetus, his crash an epiphany. Covered in mud and with a mouthful of muck after falling into a ditch, for Marinetti, this was living and it had to be savoured.[24] The impetus seemed to be to mobilize the staid air. What if one could penetrate it, whisk their way through it? The Futurists' *Aeropittura*, or aeropainting, would seek to achieve this in images, as seen in the work of Tullio Crali's *Dogfight* (1938). Thomas Pynchon's character Kit expresses this appeal as their flight nosedives into the perspectives Crali would render. Moving hellward, the Futurists portrayed 'Pure velocity. The incorporation of death into what otherwise would only be a carnival ride.'[25] Some wanted to solidify the air into something accessible, more permanent and everlasting. Even writing would follow, with Saint-Exupéry turning away from his more 'romantic' and aqueous manner. He was beginning to depart from what he saw as the 'exaggerated' and 'overblown' towards a heavier and less vaporous style, moving away from the more Impressionist imaginations, which, as in Monet and Carlo de Fornaro, made the air an envelope, a soft and cushioning membrane to perceive the world. The movement is instead towards something more forceful, to blast through it with light, colour and acceleration.

Such a brand of solidity sounds counterintuitive. Even the balloon, which inexorably drifts, hanging there in space, was often tethered. Public rides had been a permanent fixture since the balloon-mania or madness of the late 1780s. Victorian spectators arrived at a demonstration, 'craning'.[26] That tilting to the air would develop what was called the 'aerial neck', the troublesome condition of neckache caused by spectators searching upwards into the sky, wide-eyed or squinting to make out distant shapes against the clouds or the sun's glare.[27] The widespread public display of the aeroplane was surely quite a different

Carlo de Fornaro, *America's Tallest Tower, Plus Some Temperment*, 1914, photomechanical print.

Camille Grávis, *Captive Balloon with Clock Face and Bell, Floating above the Eiffel Tower, Paris, France,*
c. 1880, watercolour over graphite underdrawing.

embodiment of the balloon, but maybe the skyscraper was somewhere betwixt and between? The skyscraper might have made more permanent the anchoring line from the balloon to the ground, except that the balloon is not fast, but a steady and possibly more stable platform. The motion does not appear to be ecstatic, or necessarily uplifting or scary. It is more contemplative and 'largely silent'. This quality meant the balloon became a valuable asset in warfare, perhaps first in 1794 when the French Revolutionary Army faced a coalition of Austrian and Dutch forces in Fleurus, Belgium. A scientist, Jean-Marie-Joseph Coutelle, employed L'Entreprenant to oversee the battlefield. Outside the relative stability of the balloon's space, from afar these floating shapes – in war – were intimidating aerial figures.[28]

If Lawrence's bike could blast away the stagnant and slow air, then design could build over and up to it. Le Corbusier and Bel Geddes, both inspired by flight, would lead an architectural aesthetic never to return to ground below. This was a design that could cleanse urban squalor and airbrush the social blemishes of the cities.[29] Life in the air seemed to be living a modern vertical fantasy that would later flatten into the air-conditioned suburbs of the postwar period.

Outdoing the new skyscrapers of the New World, Paris would boast a truly aerial monument. The Eiffel Tower, which was built for the Paris World's Fair in 1889, drew on the materials and technologies that would characterize America's airborne colonization. Without the right angles of the skyscrapers, the tower did it in style. The curving legs almost proved impossible for elevator companies to install their lifts, including the famous Otis whom Eiffel eventually employed. For one American journalist, the tower was 'distinctively French. It kisses its finger tips at you. It is nothing if not light, airy, volatile. It strikes one as being even effervescent.'[30] With nothing else to compare it to, commentators struggled to find apposite metaphors for the experience. Seeing the air of its upper platforms as 'bracing' and healthy, the figure of the ship stuck. *Le Figaro* compared the structure to a city hanging in the rigging of an immense steamer. The wind gusts came fresh and sharp like the sea breeze; one might take the sky, seen through the iron bars, for the perspective of the endless ocean.[31]

The Eiffel Tower Attracts Electrical Atmospheres, 1902.

Thomas Alva Edison
and Adolphe Salles
standing on a balcony of
the Eiffel Tower, 1889.

Eiffel himself, however, could see the tower helping the world's scientists garner greater knowledge about the air itself.[32] This might be the workings of 'atmospheric currents', the 'chemical composition of the atmosphere', the variations of temperature at varying heights, and a number of different experiments not normally permitted because of the poor air quality or low-lying mist on the ground below, including a wind tunnel. Paul Langevin, who would become Marie Curie's lover, scaled the tower to perform electrical experiments on the atmosphere. Even Vernier radio signals would be transmitted from the top of the tower in order assess the atmospheric effects on radio waves.

A little earlier, air and vertical living had met more silently underground and encased as infrastructure within Holly's 'steam heat' system for New York City. In 1881, Birdsill Holly patented

the first steam radiator, which gave way to a series of other advances as he forged ahead with a district steam heating system for downtown Manhattan. The system was fed by a vast boiler topped by a 64-m-high (210 ft), 9.75-m-across (32 ft) untapered chimney on Courtland and Washington, a new landmark for New York in 1882 as passers-by wondered at the workmen-cum-flies scrambling up the tower to complete it. Falling from the dizzying heights was the furthest thing from their minds.

What later became the 'New York Steam Company' fed heat and power to New York's skyscrapers and apartment

Alexandre Gustave Eiffel's air laboratory and wind tunnel at the Champ de Mars, Paris, 1910.

New York's Steam Heat.

buildings by an underground network of pipes conveying their steam into a hive of businesses, industries and residences. Could it have gone unnoticed that the very powered air which gave speed to transatlantic migration by the 'steamers' was now permitting the colonization of the skies? From the Empire State Building, Chrysler, Tudor City to Radio City at the Rockefeller Center, steam heat promised all the benefits of living in the air. No boiler plants, smokestacks, grime or exhausts, the system tingled with the city planner's vision of air and sunlight. Steam heating meant steam ironing, steam printing for the high-rise newspaper presses, and feeding Rockefeller's new plaza, the opera that was planned would also give way to radio and later television – a perceptibly more 'democratic' business according to the *New York Times* – as

Eytinge Soloman,
*The Hearth-stone of
the Poor – Waste Steam
Not Wasted*, 1876,
wood engraving.

The meterological equipment housed at the weather station on the Eiffel Tower, 1900.

sunlight, air, and the airwaves came together in an efficient modern machine of circulation.

The atmospheric changes in New York did not prove uneventful because steam-heat was considered an intolerable nuisance, although for many others, even the urban poor, it was a blessing. Subterranean Manhattan was routinely opened up in the Company's often disruptive digging. 'Who owns Broadway, anyway? Does the New York Steam Company or the City of New York?', exclaimed an angry and perspiring Gothamite in 1889, who was enveloped in a humid cloud during the maintenance of a steam pipe.[33] This leakage was also permanent. Wisps of steam escaping manhole covers added atmosphere as the hot pipes occasionally leaked or touched colder water from broken water services with sizzling evaporation. Sometimes the streets turned into geysers of hot expulsions of air that could reach five storeys high, blowing manhole covers, falling as rain and clumps of mud. Cracks and

fissures appeared in the pavement that bulged and bellied in a volcanic illusion, mist obscuring the street.

In 1927 Lindbergh would return triumphant to the same city, having successfully crossed the Atlantic. He was given a ticker-tape parade on a day that was to become known as the 'blizzard' of Manhattan. Ticker tape was the ribbon-length paper on to which the Stock Exchange's 'ticker' machine printed telegraphed stock quotes. Manhattan's streets routinely became canyons of people, air and paper, as the air currents between the buildings swirled in the vortices and updrafts during moments of public celebration and exhilaration.

Lindbergh's snowstorm of tickertape, 1927.

The Humors of the Presidential Campaign in New York City, 1888, wood engraving.

Falling from the windows, the ticker tape performs a little like Marey's rippling threads of vapour. Almost 4.5 million people came to the island and 1,800 tonnes of the ribbon was provided. The light filtered through the rolling atmosphere of fluttering paper, coming to fall on the ground and grouping into drifts of tape. It

69

was a snowstorm of triumphalism, technological modernity and the fulfilling of America's destiny of flight, prophesying the spiritual improvement of life on earth. Of course, the Wall Street Crash of 1929 would dramatically burst this inflationary gesture, made in part by the exhausted waste (ticker tape) of New York's financial services.

These vertical oneiric fantasies, made real to the airborne, would mirror the changing understanding of the inner mind. Manhattan's aviators, skyscrapers and modern engineering of air, become a more fitting model for a Jamesian rather than Freudian unconscious. Between them was Freud in the interior world of his dark, book-cramped study, and James in the class-room looking out of the window. America's new aerial life was a 'kind of outdoors', an open to expand into. William James would give a series of talks before the end of the century to college leavers or school graduates, titled: 'Talks to Students on Life's Ideals'. In his essay eventually named, 'On a Certain Blindness in Human Beings', James sought not a sentimental message, but more of a lament of what he saw in middle-class values centred on materialistic and consumerist goals.[34] Quoting Robert Louis Stevenson, James urges his listeners not to

> miss the personal poetry, the enchanted atmosphere, that rainbow work of fancy that clothes what is naked and seems to ennoble what is base; in each, life falls dead like dough, instead of soaring away like a balloon into the colors of the sunset; each is true, each inconceivable.

'To miss the joy is to miss all', James reminds us. Yet this ascensional gesturing is not about the rush to the world. James was suggesting instead that the psyche had to welcome the world and its wonders, balloons, rainbows – the most simple and superfluous of things. The air, writes Ann Douglas, 'had been not shut out but let in'.[35] From the skyscraper and in the confidence of architectural modernism, one should throw open the windows and doors.

2 An Excess of Air

Ugly, foul, squalid, the air works on all men.[1]

A story of air must inevitably be a story of encounters with difference. One of the problems of understanding air was making sense of its lack of uniformity. Some air was hot, some cold; some air was good, some bad. Humoral theory led the way as it had with Hippocrates and his identification of unwholesome air. The salubrity of air began to be understood as a measure of its toxicity or purity for breathing, but it went further than that. Joseph Priestley had a hand in its development by identifying the 'goodness of air', and thus aligning the qualities of air with virtue. Air that had been vitiated (exhausted of oxygen) could be potentially restored and, thus, made breathable and virtuous again, as explored by Priestley in a range of experiments from 1774 to 1799. A variety of technologies were developed in England, France and Italy, but the eudiometer was the brainchild of the Italian Marsilio Landriani, professor of experimental physics at the Scuole Palatine in Milan. In his *Physical Investigations on the Salubrity of Air*, published in 1775, Landriani evolved both the equipment and theory of Priestley's initial observations. His design for the eudiometer, derived from the Greek word *eudios* or 'goodness of air', could measure the degree of respirability of a climate and, thus, its influence on the body. Carried by the wave of his invention, he announced that it could lead to a new discipline of aerial medicine.[2] Yet the divination of air's goodness was soon to be expelled.[3]

Tav. 2

Fig. 1.

Fig. 2.

Fig. 3.

Fig. 4.

Fig. 5.

Fig. 6.

By developing a quantitative method to objectively measure air, Alessandro Volta's later combustion technique would explore the relative inflammability of air and help to split the salubrity of air's virtuousness from the question of whether it was actually harmful to breath. With research conducted mostly in France and Italy, Volta could be found collecting marsh air from rotting matter at the bottom of ditches and Lake Como. At the bottom of the lakebed, Volta captured the gases using an inverted glass jar. With his modified eudiometer, Volta would run a current through the gases to ignite them before measuring the remaining material. Following Volta's findings, in 1783 the Portuguese scientist Jean-Hyacinth Magellan would write to Priestley and explain that 'I do not mean, that, by eudiometrical experiments we are enabled to discover all the bad qualities of the atmosphere, but only those of its phlogistication'. Simply put, the eudiometer could not make judgements on an air's moral and spiritual wholesomeness.

Unwholesome urban

Until this point, the humours had dominated many interpretations of city air. Perhaps the most notable is John Evelyn's *Fumifugium* (1661), a warning of the 'unwholesome air' of Whitehall that was threatening the health of London and its people forced to breathe 'but an impure and thick mist, accompanied with a fuliginous and filthy vapour, which renders them obnoxious to a thousand inconveniences, corrupting the Lungs' and their bodies. Dr Thomas Tryon in 1668 would similarly discuss the 'Moyst air' of London, 'where various sorts of Filth and Uncleanness are heaped up' to the extent that they agitate the internal feelings of the body, the air 'fill'd with foul fulsome vapours of pernicious qualities'. The seventeenth-century city was best expressed in the language of putrid atmosphere. Certain air implied immoral behaviour, vice, prostitution, bribery, theft and rumour. Ultimately, stench, 'sex and soot' were the markers of a polluted city and the polluting degeneracy of the populace.[4] By the eighteenth century the

Marsilio Landriani,
Eudiometer, 1775.

countryside took on more of the qualities of a rural idyll – the philanthropist Jonas Hanway idealizing the country where one 'can suck in the ambrosial air'. Countryside and cottages were portrayed outside the stagnation of the city and its dangerous airs. John Constable's studies of landscapes, clouds and skies reflected one another in the Romantic yet almost scientific precision that he would use to express meteorology and rural life.

John Constable, *Study of Clouds above a Wide Landscape*, 1830, pencil and watercolour on laid paper.

Paris would undergo its own 'Great Stink' when 'death was in the air, and it smelled like excrement'.[5] The public cried, 'The odors are truly unbearable'; 'We've never seen anything like this!'; 'This can't go on!', and the scientists all agreed.[6] Even though the state's responsibility towards sanitation was taken beyond the humoral and pneumatological concern for virtue or

Paul Fürst, *Doctor Schnabel von Rom*, 1656, engraving.

insalubrity towards germ theory, by the 1850s Galenic influences were still present in the stubborn theories of miasma. Miasmas would explain the spread of disease and pestilence by air which would work their way into the minds of public health reformers such as Edwin Chadwick in London. Miasmic theory had dominated Europe's understanding of the transmission of plague through 'corrupted air' by Spanish Muslim physicians and Italian academics Jacme d'Agramont and Gentile da Foligno, who wrote the tract *Consilium contra pestilentiam* in the fourteenth century. According to Foligno, corrupted air spread the plague by infecting and reinfecting other bodies through the inhalation and later exhalation of poisonous vapours, or what would be known as plague's 'seed'. Despite the prevalent imaginary of a cosmic or divine cause for plague, Foligno indeed proffered that earthquakes, tremors and various other earth movements might release corrupted airs from caverns and pockets of air hidden within the earth, pointing out that an earthquake had struck Italy a few months before the plague in 1347. Of course, these ideas would manifest themselves in the Plague doctor and the image of his mask – a beak that was stuffed with aromatic spices to counter the miasma. In spite of eventual advancements, disease remained airborne and therefore smell-bound to stench. For the Victorian reformer Chadwick, 'all smell is disease.'[7]

In eighteenth-century Paris, the thoroughly contaminated and unbreathable air threatened the biological future of the local population and, by extension, of the nation itself. The agenda was especially moralizing. Commentaries of France's urban poor recorded many different kinds of bad air, the smell of 'stale, nauseating odor, [the] slightly acrid odor of filth, odor of garbage, odor of bodies, etc., etc.'[8] Born into this stink was Jean-Baptiste Grenouille, the despicable and fictional character of Patrick Süskind's *Perfume*.[9] Grenouille embodies everything that was twisted about the corrupt Parisian air.[10] Grenouille was born or dropped into the most putrid spot of all, where the stink was almost a viscous form – it could be 'squeezed', lying 'leaden' in the alleys. And in this regard, Süskind is excavating the kinds of moral and medical concerns for air that had pervaded as 'spoilt' and 'ill boding'.[11]

If women were supposed to be disposed to smell, the lowest of the senses, it was men like Grenouille who would sniff them out. His mind was a perfect catalogue, a vast universe of boxes and rooms for the kaleidoscope of different odours, perfumes and a universe of combinations of smell. It was the place where the women or girls he murdered so carefully were archived, catalogued and possessed. As if a eudiometer, Grenouille's nose was the instrument of his eyes and imagination. Grenouille's evident hunger for the air he harvested was as a starving animal right from birth. Take this scene, as Father Terrier watches Grenouille – then but a baby – awaken from sleep,

> Its nose awoke first. The tiny noise moved, pushed upwards, and sniffed. It sucked air in and snorted it back out in short puff . . . Father Terrier, was that target. The tiny wings of flesh around the two tiny holes in the child's face swelled like a bud opening a to bloom . . . It seemed to Terrier as if the child saw him with its nostrils, as if it were staring intently at him, scrutinizing him, more

Samuel Bough, *View of a Manufacturing Town*, 1886, watercolour.

piercingly than eyes could ever do ... The child seemed to
be smelling right through his skin, into his innards. His most
tender emotions, his filthiest thoughts lay exposed to that
greedy little nose.[12]

While Terrier shuddered as Grenouille sniffed his way to his
soul, the same greedy vigilance would be turned back to the city,
the air a potential suspension of bodily emanations, the urban
streets almost an inner chamber of frightening compositions of
smoke, oils and vapours, exhalations, fermentations and miasmas.

'Fluff?' said Margaret, inquiringly.
'Fluff,' repeated Bessy. 'Little bits, as fly off fro' the cotton,
when they're carding it, and fill the air till it looks all fine
white dust. They said it winds round the lungs, and
tighteneds them up. Anyhow, there's many a one as works
in a carding-room, that fall into into a waste coughing and
spitting blood, because they're just poisoned by the fluff.'[13]

It was in the bowels of industry that air would achieve some of
the excesses of immorality and ill-health. Rendered visible in
the nineteenth-century portrayal of Britain's northern industry
by writers such as Elizabeth Gaskell and Charles Dickens, in
the choking air of Gaskell's 'Darkshire' (standing in for Britain's
Lancashire cotton and textile industry), fluff takes an aerial and
poisonous form. In the extremes of heat and humidity of the
mills, the suspended fluff and cotton dust from the looms stands
as a threatening atmosphere to the population's health. The
factory's miasmic spatial metaphors of contagion take hold as air
became an obvious signature of the commoditization of the
body and its 'sweated' labour by capital. This is an air endurable
only to a 'degraded' class for Frederick Engels whose investigations
were published in 1844. Air is 'corrupted', 'poisoned', 'pestilent';
an atmosphere 'penned in as if with a purpose', forcing the poor
into conditions which are 'incomprehensible'.[14]
    Engels sees that it is the factory which produces the very
worst kinds of atmospheres, the air infused with the integral

inequalities of the capitalist system. The workers are surrounded by the worst excesses of bad air and waste, forcing them into a circle which constantly spurs them 'to the maddest excess', to the only 'two enjoyments at their command', sex and alcohol. In the industrial environments of the cotton empires of Lancashire in Britain, Massachusetts in the United States and the large development of cotton mills in Mumbai, steam not only drove the mill machinery but decreased thread breakages. Unfortunately, steam also created stifling humid conditions, and was the breeding ground for the spread and transmission of disease. Shuttle kissing, a practice which saw cotton spinners threading the cotton onto the shuttle by sucking on the cotton to draw it through the shuttle's eye, would also cause numerous respiratory diseases such as byssinosis. Weavers could 'kiss' the shuttle as many as 300 times per day. Along with poor ventilation arrangements, conditions were not improved until factory inspectors could apply public health legislation towards the end of the century.

The implied 'kissing' of the shuttle would resonate with other insinuations of the factory air. By the 1840s, the excessive temperatures of the mill, the Factory Commission in Britain would argue, had produced an environment so unhealthy that it resembled the climate of the tropics. These airs were believed to have a physically and morally degenerative effect on workers by 'their heated atmosphere'.[15] In the official report, the hot air of the mills is to blame for the outbursts of moral and social delinquency, conspiring in the early sexual development of the female population. In tropical air, puberty was supposedly brought on by the atmospheric 'excitements'. Left unchecked by moral and social discipline, this would 'inevitably lead to the ultimatum of desire'.

In its streets, factories and houses, the city seems to dangerously collect unwholesome unhealthy air. In the country, ventilation is simple. Bad air was trapped and so were the people in those imprisoned urban airs: 'How could it be possible, under such conditions, for the lower classes to be healthy and long lived!' Engels exclaimed. The likely results were misery, increased mortality and, being 'weakened by bad air', the worker would easily fall into the temptation of drunkenness and debauchery. Was it even possible for the entire city to be raised to the temperatures of its factory? Luke Howard's research into the urban atmosphere would find evidence for what today we might call the 'heat island' effect or 'urban canopy'.[16] Discovering that a city like London demonstrated 'excess' temperatures, Howard thought that this might be attributed to the conglomerations of people and industries – like busy bees – churning out air and gases to the city, from fires and chimneys, foundries, breweries, for example. Howard supposed that these emanations could account for the city's warmer climate compared to its hinterlands in the winter, and in the summer, an excess of warmth which failed to be radiated back to the sky.

Air unfamiliar

Finding his hut hotter than a furnace, Rudyard Kipling is forced out into the 'fetid night air' that seems 'almost cool'. Kipling's 'The City of Dreadful Night' is a story so evocative that 'We pant in the air which is no air, we sicken for the evanescent breath of dawn.' His narrative mirrors the miasmic and disease-ridden understandings of the polluting urban air in Europe, amplified in these more uncertain atmospheres of the colonial city which had seemed transported to London, Lancashire or Paris. The night of Kipling's story is 'thick and greasy', a surface of sliding and 'rolling' iniquity and vice, where everything is 'shut in'. His walk through Calcutta is impossible without 'encountering muck'; the air of the tenements feeling 'heavy' with a 'faint, sour stench'. Smell and odious atmospheres are not to be missed by Kipling. In fact, this bad air appears to stand in as an expression of something beneath the surface, underlying, a diagnosis of the health of the city's ill with caste wars and religious sectarianism. Population disaffection is tied up in sanitation, urban planning and the tribulations of colonial government. For Kipling, air is the 'essence of long-neglected abominations' grown rotten or putrid and requiring urgent treatment.

Air perhaps above all else marks our arrival in somewhere unfamiliar, a location perceptibly different, a way perhaps for travellers 'to concretize their deep unease – a sense that all around them, permeating everything, was difference'.[17] Classic travelogues and anthropological treatments of colonial travel are some of the best examples of the unfamiliar sense of air, repeating a trope of arrival and discomfiture. In nineteenth-century travel literature, European ways of seeing consistently render the air sensible in a particular way. India is all 'heat and dust', crowds, unwholesome and wanting. During the British Raj, air would even characterize the inequalities of a caste system which inscribed polluting airs on a sub-caste. Bad air generally meant excrement, and through the lens of colonial and class divides, it seemed that defecation was 'everywhere'.[18] Air is expressed as fever and stagnation, merging burgeoning scientific discourse over the spread of disease, social attitudes towards morality, sexuality and gender and a fearful colonial rule mulling over governmental techniques to treat the health, hygiene and disorder of public life. The enmity, or, more accurately, blindness, towards the urban poor is an issue we will return to. In fact, air did not necessarily help the traveller understand what had produced the offending atmosphere in the first place. More than likely, the visitor was smothered in disgust and an immediate sense of otherness.

In the marketplaces of Cairo or Baghdad in the 1850s, bazaars and cafés of a special kind of oriental atmosphere were to be found, unfamiliar and alien to Western explorers, magical. The airs were seducing and enthralling. While in 1832 Europe's newsreaders learn of a Madras Brahmin who 'sat in the air', levitating, the air of the oriental city worries its visitors with exposure, the thrill of a steamy air tipping over into insalubrious, unwholesome danger. In these sorts of terms, Cairo would be particularly well covered in *fin de siècle* travel narratives. De Guerville's visits to the country in *New Egypt*, published in 1905, perfectly illustrate a frantic 'toing and froing' between

the air's seductive affections that quickly begin to sicken.[19] The important encounter here is the meeting of airs and genders because nothing disturbed oriental atmospheres quite like a woman. From Gustave Flaubert's detailed accounts of prostitutes, women's movements, hips, sweat, perfume, hair and voice come to permeate oriental air. Jean-Léon Gérôme's (1863) *The Dance of the Almeh* is a classic representation expressing much of the desire and sexuality present in the oriental atmosphere. Belly dancers move with titillating excitement, gyrating, 'their flesh quivering, the scent of their bodies in the air, their harsh cries joined to wild music'. De Guerville's description comes from an encounter. He had been led by a donkey farmer into a house near the market, and sat on a small stool in a chamber lit by two smoky lamps. Charmed by three women who 'advanced, retired, returned', he was soon 'overcome'.[20]

   In those early travelogues, air was a projection, a geographical imagination of the far off materialized in text or image for meditation back in London or Paris, where Charles Baudelaire feels the pull of an air fragrant with desire that is longed for as feminine. He breathes 'the warm scent' and sees the invitation

Jean-Léon Gérôme, *Dance of the Almeh*, 1863, etching.

Daniel Gardner, *The Three Witches from Macbeth*, 1775, gouache and chalk.

of 'shorelines spreading out for me'.[21] The exotic fragrance leads as if it were a hand gently tugging one forwards; 'verdant tamarind's enchanting scent' fills his nostrils and swirls his brain. Perhaps not to be trusted fully, the titillating air of the Orient is almost that of a harpy's call. In 'Head of Air', flowing hair becomes an atmospheric mixture of air, perfume, spirit and dangerous seduction. A 'Hemisphere' of hair is the other title of Baudelaire's prose poetry in *Paris Spleen* first published in 1869. Like the air of hair in *The Flowers of Evil*, he cements the sense that the ethereal aroma is a transported space of movement. As if on a ship, one is carried away 'to sweeter climates, to blue, where the air is sweet'.[22]

Portent yet airy accounts of women were nothing new in Europe. Drawn out within other gendered imaginations of speech and smell, the figure of the female witch in history is revealing. The airs of a witch are transgressive, their speech expresses thoughts and feelings in contrast to the 'fasting from speech' that was considered more appropriate for women.[23] Witches would seduce with their melodic words but cause trouble by their meaning. They possessed a keen sense of smell, characteristics known to anyone familiar with Germanic storytelling or their substantial involution through children's writers such as Roald Dahl. In command of stewing and boiling liquids and vapours, witches were believed to discharge foul odours infecting their surroundings and those nearby. They could even control the elements. The witch seems the 'sensory inverse' of the female saint, who is restricted by fasting and celibacy, the witch aspiring to male authority and a gluttony of sins. Georgiana, Duchess of Devonshire, is again caricatured, but this time arriving from the air as a witch – one of the three from Shakespeare's *Macbeth*, alongside her socialite friends Elizabeth Lamb and Anne Seymour Damer in a work painted by Daniel Gardner in 1775. Perhaps they are chanting the three crones' lines, 'fair is foul, and foul is fair: Hover through the fog and filthy air'.

In the nineteenth century, we find that the travel writers' sensual excitability at the new air soon cools off. Renderings of exotic, sensual women begin to solidify and their air takes shape in the form of fat, held as putrid skin and wobble in wretched bodies lascivious for the coin of a Western visitor. In Cairo, even de Guerville's testimony poses the oriental women's bodies as a 'pleasant impression' but temporarily, the exception to the rule of their revolting nakedness. Elsewhere he describes a woman- 'mountain' on a donkey whose form disappears under her 'flesh'. Eustace Reynolds-Ball's famous 1857 account of Cairo is probably most interesting in the way it investigates several important mixtures of the city's atmosphere comparable with Walter Benjamin's evocation of aura. She analyses the displays of the belly-dancing Ghawazee girls at local cafés, a 'substratum of Oriental life and atmosphere' formed through the 'endless gyrations of a stout young woman of unprepossessing feature'. The dancer's movements are endlessly and tiresomely repeated as another girl, who goes through the same motions, then takes up her place.[24]

Reynolds-Ball highlights the efforts of artists attempting to assimilate place into product, but she cannot help but compare the atmospheres of the places with the first works to have come out of the Orient, such as *The One Thousand and One Arabian Nights*. Already exposed to Western mediation and intervention, the 'local colour and atmosphere' of Cairo could only suffer ruination by 'enterprising Greeks and Levantines' who were managing the Ghawazee dances for European visitors and producing as ordinary a display as any café in 'Antwerp' or 'Amsterdam'. The local artists lacked the aptitude for anything 'striking', any quality of 'originality' or 'freshness', she argues. Like Benjamin's description of the 'spark of contingency', the 'magical value' of an authentic presence, the positive values of oriental air or aura are seen to be declining through their repro- duction and the loss of originality. Familiar with the 'picture exhibitions' of Cairo's interiors and street scenes, visitors like Ball would be disappointed with only the 'faint suggestion of Oriental atmosphere' as the 'painfully modern-looking city' could be mistaken for anywhere else. 'Something about them', she writes, had been vacated.[25]

Those sentiments were not only reserved for the atmospheres of moving women with sashaying seductive bodies, but men's too. Constance Gordon-Cumming captures some of this sense of awe and disgust held by the moving 'sweating, foaming and filthy bodies' of the whirling dervishes that confront her. Her description sees the group sway from side to side, to and fro, their bodies rolling and groaning out. And then, suddenly, 'with violent, spasmodic jerks' the men were 'dashing themselves, backwards and forwards, they touch the ground with their hands, and their wildly dishevelled hair tosses right back in our faces'.[26] Reynolds-Ball had a different spin on the twirling dervishes whose motion has the 'air of a genuine mystic', and later, 'the air of the wonder-seer'.[27] Something happens in the tumultuous space between dervish and spectator, as if a drug. This is a purer and apparently far more authentic oriental dance.

Undoubtedly, Reynolds-Ball is a fussy inspector of Cairo's atmospheric charms and vices, but let us not forget that Eustace was already a distinguished expert on air and its moral and physiological wholesomeness. She was well known for her writing on the health resorts of Europe, and perhaps the beginning of *The city of the caliphs* is as good an indicator as any of her concerns for salubrious airs. The opening lines to her book describe Cairo's airs from *Arabian Nights*, 'soft – its odours surpassing that of aloes-wood, and cheering the heart'.[28]

The air of that terrible night

> The air of that terrible night, the night of poison
> When the death merchants rifled our guiltless people
> Coughing, shrieking, wailing, screams . . .[29]

If air has been explored as a dangerous and contaminating flow of unwholesomeness, disease and immorality, then perhaps twentieth-century air was marked by even far greater uncertainty. Rafatul Hussaini's poem evokes an encounter in Bhopal, India, in 1984, as the panicking residents of a toxic gas leak begin to feel the cloud. Their pain becomes indistinct from one another. The air, again, becomes the intensity of terror as well as the thing they are trying to flee. In Don DeLillo's *White Noise*, the air of the toxic cloud that has resulted from a chemical spill seems to denote an uncertainty, an unreality that Jack Gladney finds himself in, an ambiguity that moves with and inside the cloud's rolling structure and the long-term health effects of the exposure.

The Gladneys come across it and the surprise is that it is almost fixable, no longer a rumour, the cloud has formed a black billowing shape. The passengers' bodies react as they bend their necks to look outwards for a clear vantage point.[30] The event is temporarily caught in the clear beams of army helicopters whose powerful lights cast small suns onto the dark form. Tracked by the military and the passersby of cars, the cloud is packed full of chemicals but no one knows what they are. The evacuation of the city is spectacular, part of the grandness of a 'sweeping event', a scene of 'people trudging across the snowy overpass with children, food, belongings, a tragic army of the dispossessed'.[31]

Beyond humours, miasmas and germ theories, the Bhopal disaster and DeLillo's representation of a gas leak in *White Noise*, appeal to the complexity of an unruly air, excessive and uncontainable. Hussaini was writing about the worst industrial accident in history, which killed some 3,000–10,000 people by many estimates – and caused over half a million injuries in the densely populated city of Bhopal. Failing to relocate their 'obnoxious industries' outside the city, Bhopal's Union Carbide chemical plant malfunction released a toxic gas cloud which spread through the neighbouring area and communities. In *White Noise*, we face a reality that merges with a world of scientific modelling, simulations that do not quite catch up with real events, the practices of data massaging and accounting for unknown variables and contingencies. The thing about both events, one fictional in *White Noise*, the other terribly real, is that getting a grip on air's complexities and consequences is incredibly difficult. The air in these contexts seems akin to the way military thinkers have described the 'fog' of war. Take Carl von Clausewitz's metaphor, which sees air as a refracting medium, distorting information, amplifying mistakes.[32] In *White Noise*, Jack tries to get some answers from the emergency services. 'How is it going?' Jack asks. 'The insertion curve isn't as smooth as we would like. There's a probability excess', the man responds.[33]

What does it mean to have too much probability? How can there be too much? Toxic air expresses itself in the impenetrable language and practices of the SIMUVAC (the Simulated Evacuation scientists). There is too much in his exposure to both the toxins and the statistics generated by the science. He generates 'big numbers'; the scientist explains that they're 'getting bracketed numbers with pulsing stars'. 'What does that mean?' Jack asks. 'You'd rather not know', the scientist replies.[34]

Research on the Bhopal disaster evokes the same futility. The situation is still in the air, still leaving the Bhopal population in a permanent state of confusion and suspense. Some had awoken to an odd smell, thinking neighbours were burning chilli peppers; they knew that something was different, maybe wrong. Soon they found their breathing laboured. Some quickly fled, but because there were no evacuation plans or even any information, many simply ran back into the gas or alongside it rather than away. For Kim Fortun, who was struggling to fully understand the disaster and its legal ramifications, air was an apt metaphor for the smokescreening of the events and those responsible. Bhopal would come to seem 'more like a whirlwind – a maelstrom produced by opposing currents, sucking everything into an upward spiral – with gas victims at storm center'.[35]

The company responsible for the leak was half-owned by American Union Carbide Limited, 22 per cent owned by the Indian government and the balance by Indian citizens, which made finger-pointing a game. Union Carbide Limited claimed that an individual, which wrested responsibility for the event outside Union Carbide's control, had sabotaged the plant. Indeed, it was atmospheres that Union Carbide Limited used as evidence for this sabotage in a research paper of 1988. A primary witness used in the paper's evidence was a tea boy who observed a 'tense atmosphere' among employees just following the leak, 'thus "verifying" that all workers on-site were involved in a conspiratorial cover-up'.[36] The author of the paper drew several circles on his schema of the piping configuration of the Bhopal Plant and particularly the connections going to a storage tank. The representational move is a spherical circumscription. The scientist draws off the likely causality of the events that led to the chemicals being released into the atmosphere, closing down its likely initiation to one or two disgruntled employees. This lesson, Fortun writes, is meant to be straightforward, sealed, delimited, 'in time and space. It is finished'.

In 2007, the artist kanarinka conducted an arguably odd experiment. Jogging the entire evacuation route system of Boston, it took 154,000 recorded breaths in 26 runs to evacuate the city. The evacuation system had been installed in 2006 as part of the city's campaign to prepare itself for potential threats, be they snowstorms, terror events, hurricanes, infrastructural failure or fires. Intending to capture the 'fear' surrounding the preparedness campaign, kanarinka collected her breaths in a sculptural archive of breath made up of 26 jars corresponding to each run along the evacuation route. A speaker in each jar would play the recorded breaths. What we have in kanarinka's archive is perhaps an extension of the library of Paris air that Marcel Duchamp intimated at in his *50 cc of Paris Air* in 1919, presumably made up of the collective breaths and emanations that made up the Parisian atmosphere. Thus, these collections present us with a solution to a historical problem. For insofar as we do not have a global library of air, how can we really know what the air was like? How can we preserve the smells and sensation of the air of the past, pregnant with our moods, our talk and the food on our breath, the fleeting senses of air? The urban ecological historian David Gissen has proposed an ingenious and speculative ice-core archive of city air, namely, Manhattan's, a city whose engineers have been incredibly prolific at producing new indoor natures of comfort, escape and refuge.[37] Gissen's product modifies the ambitious 1950s Bollman map of the city's buildings stretching

The Bhopal Memorial
Statue, 2009.

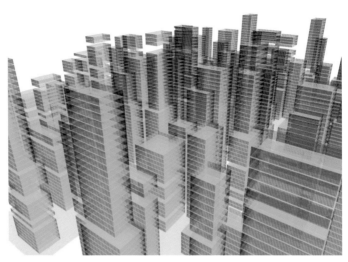

David Gissen, *Reconstruction of Midtown Manhattan*, 2002.

An Archive of Breaths, 2008, audio sculpture.

vertically into the skies, by representing the buildings almost as ice-cores. He captures Manhattan's intense indoor air production and, therefore, energy use as represented volumes of manufactured weather stacked on top of one another.

3 Restoration

This freshness is the true tonic quality of air, the one that makes breathing a joy, the one that dynamizes motionless air.[1]

A girl sits on the ground as the day passes in front of her eyes and the sun slowly descends behind the mountain. The peaks come alive, taking on the glow of the sunset's light, the grass is painted in a hue of gold, the rocks above her dazzle and almost shimmer. The girl leaps to her feet and shouts to her friend Peter. It is sunset and going, going, gone, the light is extinguished and the rocks turn from roses into a kind of grey. Heidi throws herself on to the ground and looks unhappy.

This momentary unhappiness would turn to despair as Heidi is taken away by Aunt Deta to stay with a rich family in Frankfurt. Heidi is to be a companion to the family's daughter Clara, who is confined to a wheelchair. Away from the mountains, Heidi is desperate. She feels like a prisoner. Like a bird in a cage, she cannot see the sky nor open the windows to smell the air. There are no mountains, flowers or snow in the city and the little things that remind her of the Alps bring her to tears and illness. Fortunately for Heidi, the family doctor is sympathetic. His only remedy is that she should be returned to the mountain air that would heal her. Powders and pills cannot help, her 'native mountain air' must be restored to the child and with it her health.

Heidi's return to the same setting of the sunset is different, her appreciation of the mountain atmosphere altered. As the mountainside becomes altogether aflame and 'the white snow field glowed, and rosy-red clouds' drifted across the sky, Heidi remains still. This time she is neither afraid nor shocked by the beauty. Instead, her feelings spill out as tears rolling their way

down her cheeks, like loose stones trickling down the mountain's slopes. On account of the family doctor's orders, later in the book, Clara is soon sent to the Alps to visit Heidi. Waking late the day after arrival, Clara sits in the sun, letting the soft breeze fan her cheeks; she breathes in the spiced scent of the fir trees and feels the sunshine kissing her hands and feet with warmth, never having felt such well-being before.[2]

The pure climate of Heidi's mountain home in the Engadamine, Switzerland.

Johanna Spyri's famous children's story, first published in 1880, evokes the climate of the mountainous landscapes of southern Europe. The air is undisputedly 'good' in these stories and restoring of health and spirit; it is even something prescribed by the doctor. The region where the stories are set – between East Switzerland and the western Walen and Bad Ragaz – has become known as 'Heidiland', and even a brand of mineral water, Heidiland Water, is meant to be aerated by the oxygen of the air of Heidi's homeland. The good, pure and invigorating air of the region is part of what its ski and winter resort industry depends on. The air of Heidiland even changes during summer and winter, the *summer air* or *Summerluft* should be used to fill up one's lungs, and free oneself from routine to air out one's mind. Bathing in the winter air, or *Winterluft*, is to be emancipated from the ordinary and the dull. This promotion of good air is entangled in the social and medical context of Heidi's creation, for Heidi – a child of the good air – is an emblem of air's ability to restore.

Echoing the dramatic building and design phases within the history of European health and leisure mobility to the Alps, Heidi's journey is one, we might say, of restoration – a way to resist and recuperate from the air we saw in the last chapter. Air can make one whole again.

Elevation

Friedrich Nietzsche wrote about his internal tempo, a spiritual metabolism which was driven by the environment around him. 'Make a list for yourself', he demands, of all the places where intelligent people have been. These places – Paris, Provence, Florence, Jerusalem, Athens – all of them have 'outstandingly dry air'.[3] In fact for Nietzsche, this is what genius depends on, 'clear skies' that will deliver strength and vitality to one's metabolism. While bad air was a recurrent theme and threat in the last chapter, Nietzsche makes an argument that good air does good things. His ill health would lead him to reflect on such implicit powers of recovery and restoration. As a 'very finely calibrated and reliable instrument', Nietzsche could easily interpret the effects of climate and meteorology on his health and his work. '*Sit* as little as possible', he wrote, and 'do not believe any idea that was not born in the open air and of free movement – in which the muscles do not also revel'.[4]

In Nietzsche, we find a strong almost aggressive European tradition which takes air of a high and pure character to be the right environment for the restoration of health and well-being. Baudelaire's poetics would echo this too, describing the Alpine qualities that could cleanse the spirit in his 'Elévation'.[5] As Gaston Bachelard explores in his elaboration of Nietzsche's air, there is a cultural yearning to be borne back to the air, to expand so that the spirit as well as the body might take flight.[6] What we see in these reactions to the contagious air of the lowlands are what Bachelard describes as the 'tonic' quality of air held in the peaks of the mountains and in our dreams.

There is no mistake in the timing of Heidi's materialization in Spyri's book.

The book appeared about the same time as air's assimilation into the administration of hospital and sanitation therapies and the curative architecture of the Alpine sanatorium whose resorts would see a huge amount of health and leisure tourism. Davos in the Engadin, Switzerland, was to become one of the archetypal models of Alpine design for tuberculosis patients; its particular qualities of air and sun the benchmark for the planning of other sanatoriums located in similar climates.[7] Designed by Karl Turban, the building was entirely about hygiene and the exposure of the patient to the qualities of air, light and sun.[8] The later Queen Alexandra Sanatorium, built in 1907, would take Turban's exemplar to another level of modern design, envisaged by architects Otto Pfleghard and Max Haefeli. Developments in the treatment of tuberculosis saw the open air and the sun's rays as the ideal combination for treatment of different ailments and variants of TB. Hotels and sanatoriums appeared as if out of thin air, adorned with stepped balconies and sun terraces, perfect opposites to the squalor and stagnant airs of the urban slums of Europe and North America.

This movement in Alpine sanitation design marked a wider change in the imagination of mountain climates. Gone was the mountain as forbidding, cold and dangerous, to an aesthetic which would see higher climates characterized as lands of 'light and repose'. The mountain air became curative, a strange attractor for health tourism. For the tuberculosis expert and sanatorium specialist René Burnand, sanatoriums could be well suited to take advantage of their location in high places. The air was light and invigorating and could be drunk as 'one would take in a generous wine', the atmosphere soaked with a 'mysterious power of celestial radiations', a 'white, gilded and blue enchantment, bathed in a freshness of air so curiously associated with this ardent light'.[9] Restorative treatment bound air, light and elevation together, at all ends of the spectrum, and by that I mean the wavelength of light. Heliotherapy met phototherapy as Wilhelm Conrad Röntgen was discovering x-rays and Marie Curie identified the values of radiotherapy. Preceding these treatments, the Swiss physician Arnold Rickli and other clinicians such as Auguste Rollier at Leysin and the American John Harvey Kellogg suggested that a patient should be immersed, even washed, in air and light. As part of his 'atmospheric cure' in 1855 Rickli would coin the treatment the 'atmospheric bath' – whereby patients take a soak in air, light and sun – our true elements.

Air was not just beneficial for bodily health. Even though the Alpine sanatorium became the stay for those escaping the morbidity of the city, during the cessation of war, the heights of Davos would allow Expressionist painters such as Ernst Ludwig Kirchner to find what Rousseau described as 'ease in respiration, greater lightness and agility of body, and more serenity in the mind'.[10] Kirchner travelled to recuperate in sanatoriums on several occasions following his breakdown in 1916, after signing on as an artillery driver – an attempt to avoid conscription into the German infantry. The onset of war would change Kirchner's atmospheres, no longer inhabiting the 'exotic ambience' of his Berlin studio, which resembled an 'opium den'.[11] The violence of the war installed a kind of pressure, the impression of a bloody carnival; life becomes superficial, irrelevant, ephemeral. His job, as he perceived it, was to apprehend the 'topsy turvy', to seek the something 'in the air', to find an image from the 'confusion'.

Northern Europe was not the only place for the restorative air of the late nineteenth and early twentieth centuries. Even southern California would be cast in a similar light, encouraging immigrants to the region, which had been labelled 'Nature's Great Sanitarium'. The climate was just right for the recovery of consumptive TB patients, with 'a pure atmosphere' and a 'genial sky'.[12]

Sea

Women's relationship with air was not often one of emancipation. In Jane Austen's *Persuasion* (1817), Henrietta and Anne take a turn at 'the cobb', then an often-used jetty in Lyme Regis, on the south coast of England, and a natural place to enjoy the bracing sea breeze.[13] The sea air 'always does good', with very few exceptions, according to Henrietta. So self-evidently restoring, it would do more good than 'all the medicine' in the world. This narrative soon returns to the air as a force to disturb the gaze of a man. As Anne's restored face catches a gentleman's eye, he starts to look at her with 'a degree of earnest admiration'. The gentleman notices the qualities in her face glowing now that it has been brought back to colour, 'the bloom and freshness of youth restored . . . and by the animation of eye, which it had also produced'. The admirer's gaze is further responded to by Captain Wentworth, who reciprocates the gaze back at Anne with another 'glance of brightness'.

With all this description of ardent gazes and bright glances, men enraptured by the gale force of women brought back to full health, the Victorian health resorts of Brighton, Scarborough and Blackpool would entice nineteenth-century writers with their restorative qualities of salty sea air. They would later become the context for the sexual frisson of marital affairs and the carnival qualities of a liminal zone, with the seaside positioned as it was between land and sea. As oases of health, these places could also be a chance for reflection as well as rejuvenation. At Cromer on the north Norfolk coast, Elizabeth Gaskell's Margaret Hale would seek bodily strengthening upon the death of her parents and family friend in *North and South* (1855). For Wendy Parkins, what we see here is an emerging autonomous and independent mobility of women, taking advantage of the Victorian railways extending their way to the seaside resorts, pulled in by the good air.[14] Margaret, now tragically relinquished of her father and mother, goes to Cromer. There by the sea she is quite immobile. The sea air, its breeze and other characters move about her. Margaret is there for the curing of mind as much as body. Yet hers is not

'The Accident', from *Persuasion* in collotype, 1892.

a passive submission to the air. Braced by the wind, on Margaret's return to town she takes her life into 'her own hands', and from this chrysalis a new woman is born.

Real-life women began to emulate Margaret Hale's motion to Cromer. Women would walk in Brighton and other seaside towns, designed with high-society promenades, the purpose of which was 'to breathe the sea air' and its breezes.[15] The building works of esplanades, promenades, jetties, parades, piers and terraces drew on the Mediterranean, places like Venice and especially the marina at Palermo. Signs of women's increasing freedoms were extended by the provision of cool breezes and the shelter of a shade. Indeed, 'No husband, it was said, would dream of forbidding his wife to walk at night in the shade of the marina.'[16] Social anonymity and mixing was also possible in the late evening as the marina would allow social separation to blur through the confused cloaking of identity in the failing light.

North and South is a book full of air and atmospheres which foretell Hale's modernity, while expressing a wider societal concern for a certain sort of bad air, or even the humoral temperament of melancholy which Robert Burton would so comprehensively expound in his *The Anatomy of Melancholy*, published in 1621. Melancholy was a temperament that would commonly affect the literate and artistic classes. Its airs appear thick, cloudy, foggy and impure. Melancholy expresses an air of dejecting spirit, it 'causeth diseases by infection of the heart'. Melancholic air attacks from without and within. Such are the kinds of air which plague Margaret before Cromer. They immerse her, express her moods, suffocate her mother with dampness. But there are also airs that she eventually confronts, and through that process, restores some sense of power back to herself. In Cromer, Margaret takes the air for her own, while earlier in the book in Milton she battles it. At first Margaret's relation to the air is indifference, or rather her attitude is as easy and variable as a light breeze. Margaret bathes in the environment of Helstone, her childhood home in the south. She lives in a pragmatic and ignorant state of the apprehensions and fears and worries of those around her. Any internal dissonance is quickly forgotten by a sunny day. All her cares 'blown away as

After William
McConnel, *Brighton
Beach*, 1866, engraving.

lightly as thistledown'. This soon changes as her situation is radically transformed. Her father leaves his role as a minister for a position in the north in Milton, Darkshire. The winds of change in this part of the book set up an inevitability. Unpacking the house into the rented accommodation they take at first outside Milton, Margaret sees 'a thick fog' surrounding the house. It is said to creep with searching fingers, feeling its way into the house through the windows in white, unwholesome mists.

> 'Oh, Margaret! Are we to live here?' asked Mrs Hale, in blank dismay. Margaret's heart echoed the dreariness of the tone in which this question was put. She could scarcely command herself enough to say, 'Oh, the fogs in London are sometimes far worse!'
>
> 'But then you knew that London itself, and friends lay behind it. Here – well! We are desolate. Oh Dixon, what a place this is!'
>
> 'Indeed, ma'am, I'm sure it will be your death before long, and then I know who'll – stay!'
>
> . . .

There was no comfort to be given. They were settled
in Milton, and must endure smoke and fogs for a season;
indeed, all other life seemed shut out from them by as thick
a fog of circumstance.

Things only get worse. Margaret's stupor is temporarily
suspended by their movement out of the fog into the smoke and
grimy landscape of Milton. But these airs appear more noble,
quite unlike the damp and more soulful qualities of the semi-
rural mists which insist worry onto her mother. Unfortunately,
Mrs Hale soon succumbs to some respiratory disease. Reflecting the pale fatalistic way tuberculosis was understood, in the
lead-up to her death Margaret's mother tries to hide her illness.
She believes the truth of her condition, despite outward appear-
ances, to be far worse. At this stage in the book women seem
extremely sensitive to air, fluttering like flags in a breeze, while
it is men who are set against it – against the wind. The mill owner
Mr Thornton battles the elements, he moves in spite of them
– to spite the air itself. When it is announced that Mr Thornton
is coming to tea, Mrs Hale fatalistically exclaims, 'But, east or
west wind, I suppose this man comes'. Mrs Hale and Margaret can
only wonder at the man's indifference, 'The more it rains and
blows, the more certain we are to have him.'[17]
Margaret learns to confront the air. We see this as labour
relations in Milton breakdown. This comes to a head as Mr
Thornton stands his ground in the factory forecourt as a growing mob of workers congregate to voice their dissatisfaction and
verge on rioting. Between Thornton's immobility and Margaret's
sensitivity, we can locate a gendering of air in common within a
much longer cultural history of the senses. Men were more associated with the more rational world of sight. Meanwhile, women
are understood to have a far greater sensibility of touch, smell
and taste, such as the 'smell of dinner, the touch of her husband,
and children, the scent of the flowers in the garden, the feel of
cloth and needle, and the warmth of the hearth'.[18] From more
pagan origins, it was not uncommon to believe that the womb
was in fact quite autonomous from a women's intentions – that

it had its own movement and sense of smell. Incense became a cure for gynaecological ailments. In some cases, bizarrely, a foul odour would be placed near the woman's nose and a perfume to the vagina, intended to encourage the 'keen-scented womb to travel away from the foul odours and towards the fragrance', whilst a distended womb would necessitate an opposite treatment.

In Milton, it is Margaret and not Mr Thornton who is 'struck' metaphorically by the crowd. Its motion and atmosphere are 'buzzing' with 'excitement'. The crowd takes on the 'thunderous atmosphere' of a storm which boils morally as well as physically, around her, starting in 'a low distant roar' – remember the revolutionary airs of France? Once more the turbulence builds as a volatile mixture of air and fluid, first from the 'slow-surging wave of the dark crowd', atmospheric disturbances which forced 'themselves on Margaret's notice'.[19] The crowd's bodies are turned into battering rams against the gates of the mill, the strong gates aquiver, 'like reeds before the wind'. In the standoff, and losing the moment, Mr Thornton's authority is arrested as he fails to speak or move. Folded up, his arms crossed as if a barrier and his body tight – as 'still as a statue' – his silence almost lets the raging whirlwind free. At this moment, Margaret anticipates the uproar and the possible explosion of men, boys and passions that will easily sweep beyond them. She sees some boys about to give flight to their wooden clogs, their missiles a potential spark to the unrest – perhaps taken by the devil's opportunity to agitate their spirits for 'when the humours by the air be stirred, he goes in with them'. She rushes to confront the crowd. Margaret's effect is an almost equal and opposite force, her air is vacated but it halts the tide, causing the atmosphere to waver.

> For she stood between them and their enemy. She could not speak, but held out her arms towards them till she could recover breath.[20]

Disciplining air

Could air be enough to cure, to bring the body back to full health on its own? The emerging urban and medical sciences being drawn up around hygiene and the living conditions of city populations were working with a slightly different problem. Their concern was to prevent the body from succumbing to the dangerous and sickly airs of the miasmic and germ-ridden environment. At the same time, new and restorative forms of air management were taking place, where utmost importance was given to the disciplining of the air and the body that would inhabit its volumes. Michel Foucault identified the eighteenth-century French hospital as part of the wider epochal shift in the state's relation to the population, and at the heart of a strong miasmic school of thought.[21] Whilst the hospital had once been seen as a place to go to die, it would soon change through Englishman John Howard's late eighteenth-century experiments in sanitation and the transmission of disease by air. Tenon would publish his memoirs on the Hôtel-Dieu, a hospital in Paris, in 1788, which give an indication of the reversal of the hospital's role. Unlike even the military and maritime hospitals in France at La Rochelle and Marseille, which were principally concerned with preventing the spread of disease through quarantine, the hospital began to be viewed as a location for cure.[22] Here we see the key transitioning role of the hospital and its relation to air. The air became the object of a medicalized focus which saw air less in the sense of the patient's dying spirit (compared to eudiometry). In both the hospital and the sanatorium, the discipline of the air around the body, as well as the body itself, would add up to a recipe of a cure.[23] Making this happen required medicine's shift towards the atmospheric environment in which the disease and the patient were suspended.

Tenon's involvement in the monumental redesign of the fire-destroyed Hôtel-Dieu in 1772 never came to completion. The vast drawings of a circular structure, modelled on the Colosseum in Rome, were judged to be positively necessary by Lavoisier himself. He even stated in his biography that the existing and

Tenon's ideas materializing into the plans for the Hôpital Lariboisière, Paris.

charred hospital was inadequate and 'eminently insalubrious'. Having never left the drawing board, the ideas were eventually taken up in the Hôpital Lariboisière, located on the Right Bank in the tenth arrondissement, in 1854. The drawings detailed a measure of control over the air, classifying wards and the spatial distribution of patients according to type of illness, and controlling the flows of people and matter that moved in and out of

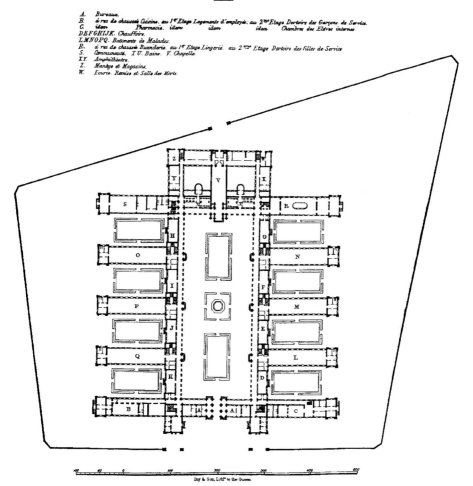

the hospital space. The patient's exposure to light and ventilated air had to be right. Even air temperature was brought under strict management. We learn of an experiment which isolated the bed of each patient using screens at the sides and the top 'that would permit the circulation of air but would block the propagation of miasmas'.[24]

The ideas were almost contagious. In Britain, the 'pavilion' plan took hold, first at the Royal Naval Hospital in Plymouth, Devon, completed in 1762, and much later in Henry Currey's monumental design for St Thomas's Hospital, finished in 1871 on the Albert Embankment on the Thames. The design emphasized above all else segregation, separation and ventilation, with each patient installed in a window pier.

The sanatorium would deploy a similar level of management over air as it began to be argued that the climatic properties of a location – places with good air becoming the resort for those with poor health – should take second seat to the proper regulation of air as medical treatment. Healthy air could be made anywhere. For the Swiss phthisiologist René Burnand, the sanatorium's methods he had deployed at Leysin could be simply and readily exported to even the Egyptian desert location of the

Henry Currey's St Thomas's Hospital, London, 1868.

al-Hayat hotel. As Guignard argues, this was possible not because air was not important, but because it only gained true 'therapeutic meaning' when it was directed by the correct methods of the sanatorium.

Back in Cromer, a little while after Margaret Hale could have visited there, the therapeutic air of Switzerland was brought to north Norfolk by the structured use of open-air treatment and phthisligistic medicine. Letting the open air in or the patient out seemed to be ideas quite opposite to the natural distrust of gusts and draughts that might leak into the house. But the place was to be Mundesley in Norfolk, and the doctor of choice, F. W. Burton-Fanning, one of the pioneers of the open-air treatment in Britain, who was publishing his work in *The Lancet* in 1898. Burton-Fanning had begun his experiments at a convalescent home, The Firs, in Mundesley in 1897. His tests were partly a success, having removed the tubercle bacillus bacterium, which could only be detected in the sputum of a few patients, and the general reduction of fever in most patients. He soon made plans to build a sanatorium on a nearby site. Fanning was greatly influenced by advances in the science of the tubercle bacteria, the treatment of TB on the Continent, and the urban physiology whose luminaries had argued that it was 'overcrowding, or, in other words, vitiated air' which bred and suspended the disease, while its virulence would be 'arrested by exposure to fresh air and sunlight'.[25] In other words, germ theory did not leave the miasmic altogether. What is more, being in a good state of health gave the patient a much greater chance of beating the infection. It was a fairly obvious statement, Fanning suggested, to assert that fresh air was good for raising a patient's general state of health.

Fanning was clearly favourable in his opinions of Mundesley, Cromer and their peculiarly healthy climates. His affection for the place was supported by evidence from other physicians who had argued that the north Norfolk coast offered a particularly dry climate, benefiting from a strong and bracing east wind and a great deal of sunshine, avoiding the 'dampness' Susan Sontag associated with many descriptions of the disease. For those Burton-Fanning treated at The Firs, he made one key proviso:

no matter how faithfully patients stuck to his advised routines in the open air, 'they were manifestly at a disadvantage as compared with the inmates of a specially appointed sanatorium'.[26] Even so, the importance of his work was justified. Most patients could simply not get to Davos or other European Alpine health resorts. For Burton-Fanning, 'the treatment must be available in their own country or nowhere.'

Bringing open-air treatment to Mundesley required a purpose-built sanatorium, a systematic method of shaping the elements around the patient within the open air, in which they should almost 'perpetually exist', and to regulate the 'strict medical supervision of the patient's daily life'.[27] Life was to be strictly controlled and strictly outdoors. The new building was of a chalet-style design, and was finished in 1899. Outdoor sheds or summerhouses, called *Liegehalle*, which the patients would inhabit during the day, dotted the grounds. The chalets needed a blind or canopy during the summer so as not get too hot, but most interestingly, Burton-Fanning employed the Norwich manufacturer Boulton & Paul to construct a turntable platform for the shelters. With this mechanism, the small structures could be turned to face away from the prevailing wind, as a means of not exposing the patients unfavourably to too much air. Following the sun's movement throughout the day would bring the additional benefits of heliotherapeutic warming – heat from the sun. As the *Liegehalle* also fell within the price ranges of the more wealthy for private use (and preceded the garden summerhouse), Boulton & Paul claimed that their chalets 'enabled the most delicate to take the utmost advantage of fresh air and sunshine, whilst strong and cold winds are excluded'.[28] Burton-Fanning prescribed that all bedroom windows should be kept open continuously, so that the air was always in motion. His methods were even intended to go beyond the sanatorium and should be trained, practised and then learned. Should the patients return to their homes, Burton-Fanning explained how the correct treatment of the body could be habitualized:

The Mundesley
Sanatorium, Norfolk.

I think a great use of the sanatorium is to thoroughly drill them in the proper habits of life. My patients have carried away with them to their homes a most intelligent comprehension of the virtue of fresh air and not only have they rigorously adhered to the prescribed mode of life, but they have also commenced to shake the rooted objections of other sufferers to pure air.[29]

Mundesley's employment of the air in a regimen of every-day routines would be repeated elsewhere, especially in the United States, where theories of ventilation had found favour, but also where the sanatorium and ventilation became a central component of municipal health. The American designs took the Mundesley model to another scale. Chicago was one of the most progressive cities to develop the sanatorium based on the open-air principles which merged the treatment of tuberculosis with other public health campaigns, especially concerns around the well-being of children. In these contexts, fresh air 'became a new weapon for the pediatric armamentarium'.[30] Chicago's Simmons Island became the site for a new purpose-built open-air

sanatorium for children and babies. Sited on an island, the sanatorium was separated from Chicago's Lincoln Park by a concrete bridge. The building was designed like a huge *Liegehalle*; a pavilion open on all sides facing Lake Michigan, easily catering for 300 babies. The city would equip these pavilions with new hammock-style beds featured in *Popular Mechanics*. The desire was for a form of bed that would be 'light, open to the air, durable, comparatively inexpensive, and capable of being washed thoroughly'.[31] The solution was as modern a solution as the suspension perambulators that sat aside the hammocks in the almost factory-like setup of the pavilion. A woven wire basket was equipped with high-flaring sides that could be suspended by ropes from two posts, as if a hammock. The hammocks could be easily removed from the supports and 'nested into compact stacks'. Yet maybe these designs were preceded by an earlier greenhouse

A view along the veranda at Mundesley.

An example of the *Liegehalle*.

One of Burton-Fanning's original turntable chalets.

A surviving shelter.

intended to preserve life: the incubator. Before they were commonplace in hospitals, the baby incubator had a curious life as a fairground and carnival exhibit. They featured on the boardwalks in Atlantic City, at Dreamland on Coney Island and at the 1904 St Louis World's Fair, where John Zahorsky's baby incubators were a major attraction on the 'pike'. Developed for neonatal care, the incubators would later be equipped to provide artificial respiration, but the first units were simply about regulating a warm ambient temperature to support the premature babies' respiratory systems and keep airborne germs away.

Louisiana Purchase Exposition, the 'St Louis World's Fair' 1904.

Chicago's Municipal Sanitarium was built for over 900 adults, featuring open-air cottages with open porches and just as ingenious modern solutions to sustain ventilation. Even the locker rooms used mesh panelling to ensure no airs were left un-wafted by the strong breeze. The city also took steps to institute the open-air principles into people's homes so that treatment could continue outside the sanitarium. In 1914, the Bureau of

Special Relief of the Dispensary Department gave provision for homes to be remodelled with outdoor sleeping areas or porches, furnished with specially designed beds, bed clothing, reclining chairs, and curtains, for example.[32]

Reclining to the sun, the sanatoriums brought air around the human body through carefully designed beds, hammocks and chairs. Their improvement on deck chairs was to almost remove as much material as possible which would be replaced by thin air. The 'cure chairs' – and Davos had its own version – made from beech, cane and wicker would be brought to the common market in the form of modernist domestic products designed for sun terraces using a tubular steel design. Thomas Mann's character Hans Castorp from *The Magic Mountain* (1924), which is set in a sanatorium in Davos, can only exclaim in gratitude at such a remarkable chair, 'What sort of chairs are they? If they are to be had here, I'll buy one and take it to Hamburg with me; they are heavenly to lie in.'[33]

Inside Zahorsky's incubator exhibit.

The sanatorium at Mundesley was interconnected with Britain's wartime and interwar artistic and literary talent; maybe

it was even a haven. Andrew Morland, a resident physician at Mundesley, and his wife Dorothy, were something of a pair within a clique of intellectual elite. Dorothy was a correspondent of D. H. Lawrence, whom they would go to visit as his health declined owing to TB. A long-time sufferer, Lawrence displayed all the characteristics that Sontag identifies in the physiological and cultural make-up of the consumptive sufferer. The failure of the lungs characterizes TB as the 'disintegration, febrilization, dematerialization' of the body that can no longer take in air. The body seems to liquefy, becoming 'phlegm and mucus and sputum and, finally, blood'; it gasps for air it cannot have, 'for better air'.[34] Lawrence's friend, the artist Mark Gertler, who had also been treated by Morland in Mundesley, helped to convince the Morlands to visit Lawrence in France, which they did in 1930 at Bandol, on the Côte d'Azur, when Lawrence was in the final stages of the illness. Dorothy spent a lot of time with Lawrence and felt that they had a common bond. The

The Tyrolean Alps at the Louisiana Purchase Exposition.

A poster campaign for the adoption of the Sanatoria Act in 1909.

MR. VOTER!

3500 FELLOW CHICAGOANS WERE KILLED LAST YEAR BY

The Great White Plague

3500 MORE ARE IN THE EARLY STAGES OF THE DISEASE AND CAN BE CURED BY CARE LIKE THIS

VOTE "YES" ON THE "LITTLE BALLOT"

AND GIVE CHICAGO THE BEST MUNICIPAL TUBERCULOSIS SANATORIUM IN THE COUNTRY

AN EMINENT SPECIALIST HAS SAID:

"We must care for the CONSUMPTIVE at the right time, in the right place, and in the right way, UNTIL HE IS CURED; instead of, as now, at the wrong time, in the wrong place, and in the wrong way, UNTIL HE IS DEAD."

IT IS UP TO YOU!

Morlands urged Lawrence, if he would not return to England, to visit the Ad Astra sanatorium in Vence, in the Alpes Maritimes, for proper medical treatment.

Earlier during the war, Lawrence and Gertler had become friends. Gertler had been a student of the influential Slade School of Drawing, Painting and Sculpture in London, along with the likes of Dora Carrington, Paul Nash and Richard Nevison.[35] Living in London at the onset of war and among the compelling personal relationships at the Slade and Bloomsbury set, Gertler found the environment to be stifling as much as it was inspiring. The contradictory forces on his state of mind and expression were all a 'whirl'. As with Kirchner, Gertler saw the war as inescapable, unavoidable and undoubtedly present. London 'overshadowed by a very large ominous cloud', the city blanketed by a 'Dead Calm' that covered everything.[36] Following a spat with fellow Slade artist Stanley Spencer, Gertler fell out almost totally with John S. Currie, who would later commit suicide after murdering Dolly Henry. Writing to Brett, Gertler would state: 'The Atmosphere he lives in stifles me . . . I want fresh Air. Real Air.'[37]

These atmospheres would lead on to Gertler's most celebrated work, *Merry-Go-Round*, in 1916, directly inspired by a funfair on Hampstead Heath in London. The work appeared as an outlet of Gertler's passions, what Lawrence would describe as his inner 'maelstrom of destruction and horror'. Gertler's most famous painting was a 'blaze' and unlike Bel Geddes's *Futurama*, whose merry-go-round, with 'boys and girls shrieking', anticipates a modern paradise of the future, Gertler's image closes off that possibility to a form of Armageddon. His vision combines 'mechanical motion and complex involution', the mouths of the riders are open, shrieking not with glee but pain. The top of the carousel appears to reflect the orange-red of a fire. The plume-like clouds around the carousel might be explosions or the shape of parachutes falling to the earth. Gertler travelled repeatedly to the Mundesley sanatorium in 1925, 1929 and 1936, to recover his bodily and mental health under Morland's care.

Following Morland's advice, Lawrence travelled to Ad Astra, where he would deteriorate further.[38] He had hoped that it would do him good, 'the air – and my wife not being worried and worrying me back again'.[39] Lawrence died on 2 March 1930 after discharging himself from the clinic and moving to Villa Robermond in Vence, Provence. Andrew Morland wrote to S. S. Koteliansky, or Kot, one of D. H. Lawrence's closest friends, a few days later. His letter appears wracked with guilt, sorry that he encouraged Lawrence to move to the sanatorium in Davos. A few years later Morland would publish a paper in *The Lancet* on 'The Mind in Turbercle'. For Morland, the treatment of a patient's mental state would help them adapt themselves most effectively 'to a suitable environment'. He attributed this to the strict 'regimen' that many patients simply would not have the endurance to maintain, should they remove themselves to the atmosphere of home, or fail to adapt sufficiently to the 'sanatarium atmosphere' either. Morland held that, of 'all the 'morbid conditions, tuberculosis is the one in which it is most essential to treat the patient rather than the disease'.[40]

4 Insulation

You've got to insulate, insulate, insulate.[1]

Overcome by something toxic in the air, a canary loses consciousness and falls off its perch. The bird's claws have been filed to prevent it remaining upright should it pass out, all because its fall was meant to catch someone's attention. Suspended in an apparatus known as the 'Haldane Box', the use of canaries in mines lasted until 1986 in the UK, until electronic detectors took their place. Their use in scientific experimentation was common, as we saw in Wright's famous image. Lavoisier had used sparrows. For the Scot John Scott Haldane, mice, birds and ultimately himself became glass-beaker subjects.

John Haldane was a remarkable man who put his body through remarkable pain, discomfort, fatigue and ultimately danger.[2] As much as he sought to discover ways to insulate and adapt the body to the dangerous airs of London's sewers and subterranean worlds of tunnels, or the realms of high altitude, he had to expose himself to dangerous air. He was to be found in sewers after engineers had died of carbon monoxide poisoning, he investigated mining disasters and he regularly exposed himself to extreme altitudes and low depths in order to understand the strange atmospheric effects on the body. Air, Haldane tried to show, was far from equal across the planet and it would have quite different effects on those who experienced it.

At altitude, one of Haldane's most important research projects was a period of work conducted at Pikes Peak, Colorado. Evangelista Torricelli had already identified the action of atmospheric pressure, using the principle of a mineshaft to design his barometer

Measuring air
exchange on Pikes
Peak in 1911,
the team's base.

in 1643, while Boyle would wonder at the differentiation of pressure at altitude within Torricelli's coined 'ocean of air'. In 1911, Haldane and a team of researchers travelled to Colorado to conduct fieldwork on the summit. They made their workplace in Summit House, positioned at a height of 4,295 m (14,100 ft) above sea level. Haldane would suffer nausea, diarrhoea, abdominal pain, periodic breathing and hyperpnoea on exertion. Others suffered worse with headaches, and everybody noticed that their lips had turned blue. The team made intensive measurements of the body's respiratory process and the comparable use of oxygen and carbon dioxide at the special altitude. They compared being in bed to being at rest. While walking the cog-wheel railway track, they used a special bag apparatus that could capture the exhaled air. The symptoms of 'mountain sickness' left the team after several days. Following Paul Bert's famous *La Pression barométrique* of 1878, the cause of these symptoms was identified as an absence of oxygen, conditions to which the team were soon acclimatized.[3]

Haldane was committed to the notion that the human body was a kind of environmental system that regulated itself. This system worked independently of the outside environment and sought to maintain 'continuous life' by producing internal conditions conducive to that state. Air naturally played a vital role in this regulation, oxygen and carbon dioxide suffused and transmitted through the blood by the respiratory system and bodily circulation. For Haldane, if the body could not be brought to breathe naturally in the dangerous aerial spaces it came to inhabit, then he would design ways of improving the body and adapting it. By improvising mechanical apparatus, Haldane brought the human body to places of dangerous, thin or heavy air. He would make improvements that provided pressurized air, cleaner and purified oxygen, or filtered out the lethal pathogens of the battlefield.

The 'bag apparatus' in use, capturing exhaled air, 1913.

Interior of the Pikes Peak laboratory, 1913.

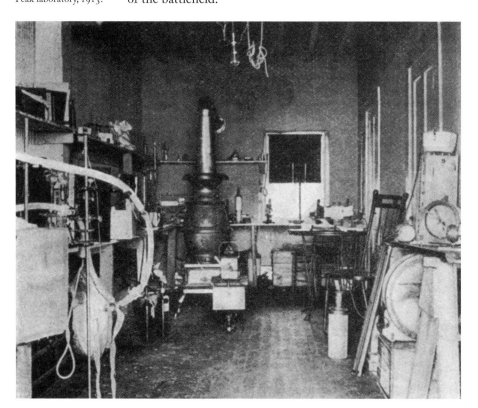

John B. Stone,
John Scott Haldane,
1902, platinum print.

In 1915 Haldane and Professor H. Brereton Baker of Imperial
College, University of London, were instructed by Lord Kitchener
to travel to Ypres in order to examine the extraordinary gassing
of over 2,000 French troops on 22 April by the release of 160
tonnes of chlorine gas. Fritz Haber's design marked an instru-
mental moment in modern warfare – a real game-changer.
Taking the environment as a means to intervene on the body, the
air was in fact weaponized to deliver incapacitation and death to
the enemy in the form of a deadly green cloud. This new weapon
worked by taking breathable air away. Gas replaced clean air so
that the aerial environment became deadly.[4]

If gas warfare was a primary expression of 'total war' – there was no surrender or escape, everyone was a combatant – it could not necessarily discriminate between friend or enemy. And yet, air has this knack of resisting intervention. Luce Irigaray's point is that air has its own internally vortical and chaotic contradictions to deal with, so that air might forget even itself and what it is intended to do. Just as the wind and the weather would intervene to blow the suspended cloud back to the German soldiers, even Haldane's recommendations on the front were constantly misinterpreted.[5] Like miners, trench tunnellers brought canaries with them but forgot what they were for. 'What about this canary', they asked, as the bird appeared lifeless and those around them started becoming drowsy. Without adequate training, his respirators were misused by soldiers who failed to provide adequate protection for themselves. And even the producers of his respirator mask had problems manufacturing it, the material carbonate of soda accidentally replaced by caustic soda, which ate through the masks and the hands of the workers manufacturing it.[6]

Haldane's personal suffering for the pursuits of science and social improvement impress for their selflessness, but at the core of his work was a kind of tension. His twin solutions could be generalized around, first, the body's protection by removal from certain air and pressures and, second, a nurturing adaptation to new conditions of air. As we will see, however, it is *insulation* that has perhaps won out over adaptation.

Air architecture

> Outside Tucson, in Arizona, in the middle of the desert, a geodesic structure of glass and metal, housing all the climates of the planet in miniature, where eight beings (four men and four women obviously) will live in total autarchy and in a closed circuit for two years – or at least that's the plan.[7]

This is how philosopher Jean Baudrillard described Biosphere 2, the 'miniaturized' experiment of earth funded by the billionaire

Texan Ed P. Bass. The project had begun much earlier in 1983 by the Institute for Ecotechnics based in Santa Fe, New Mexico. Bass had proposed a jointly funded project between his venture capital firm and the institute; the company came to be known as 'Space Biosphere Ventures'. For Baudrillard, Biosphere 2 performs an endemic catastrophism in u.s. culture. The real planet here is 'presumed condemned' and 'sacrificed' in favour of a perfected, insulated and filtered space, where there are no predators, no illnesses, no contaminations of any sort.[8] The Earth gives birth to a new perfected world, adorned with perfect atmosphere, perfect air, an 'air-conditioned clone', the space is 'artificially' immunized and its air is cleaned. No germs, microbes, no aliens; the air – everything – is purified. The sphere's sparkling exterior belies a hidden interior architecture which sustains the dome's climates. A complex system of dryers, pumps, chambers and controllers keep air circulating, organisms alive and the climate constant.[9]

Biosphere 2.

Yves Klein, *Cité Climatisée*, 1961, ink on paper.

The geodesic design of the biome might make greater sense through what we could recognize as a 'dome culture' or even bunker culture of the American futurist Buckminster Fuller.[10] Fuller's 'total thinking' and 'anticipatory design science', fulfilled in his now famous geodesic dome, was about the organization of one's environment in order to provide the most optimum allocation of resources. As contemporaries of Fuller, it was within the wider tradition of immaterial or 'air architecture' that in 1960 Yves Klein and Werner Ruhnau began their 'Project for an Aerial Architecture'. In 1958, on his 30th birthday, Klein had been given a copy of Bachelard's *Air and Dreams*, an inspiration which would see the promotion of air and the elemental in his architectural utopian projects that would do away with the predominance of existing building materials. Emphasizing protection and community, their city would be furnished with a roof made of air to condition and protect the space. Forms are made of air, in airbeds and air seats, but there is no real distinction between roof, walls or floor. The city is open and transparent and so are bodies. Everyone is naked and social structures are eradicated. This is an evolved sensibility guided by the air, by the spirit.

Yves Klein, *Air Architecture (ANT 102),* 1961.

Diller Scofidio,
the Blur building
near Neuchâtel,
Switzerland, designed
by Elizabeth Diller
and Ricardo Scofiodo.

More recent sorts of air architecture could be seen on the Lake Neuchâtel, Switzerland, in 2002. The Blur building is possibly a good example of 'air architecture' as the building is essentially a cloud that penetrates a steel skeleton of walkways and technology reminiscent of short-lived cloud camouflage techniques tested during the Second World War. Through 31,500 fog nozzles, on the lake a shape emerges to the variable dimensions above the surface of the lake of 90 m wide x 60 m (300 x 200 ft) deep and 20 m (65 ft) high. The building constantly changes shape and size, whether you are in it or outside it. However, because it is made of air and water, the building's material is its worst enemy because it is so sensitive to wind and its speed and direction, to humidity, to small climatic variances.

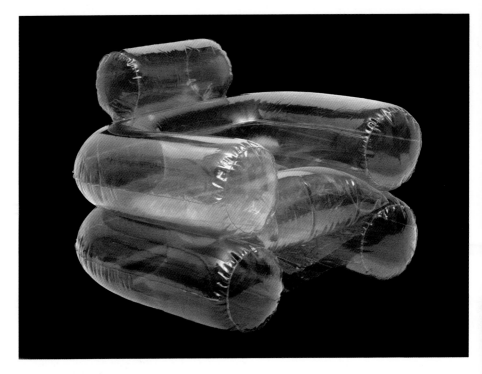

Other kinds of design would take air under a tighter if more transparent leash. Inflatable design and architecture saw the Zanotta furniture company begin to manufacture the Blow chair from 1968 using PVC sheets bonded together with high-frequency welding. Designed by Jonathan De Pas, Donato D'Urbino, Paolo Lomazzi and Carla Scolari, who would also submit a model of an inflatable structure to the Italian Pavilion for the 1970 World's Fair in Osaka, their inflatable armchair spawned a popular craze for inflatable domestic and leisure products.

Zanotta SpA, Blow Armchair, 1967.

On the one hand, then, some of the principles of atmospheric insulation have inspired inventive and experimental sorts of design which have promoted very interesting and important forms of sustainable experimentation, such as the Eden Project in Cornwall, the brainchild of Tim Smit, which opened in 2001. Or contrast with artist Mary Mattingly and her wearable home, as well as more recently, *Air-Ship-Air-City*, which includes a studio space, edible gardens, greenhouses, weather mapping and event spaces giving tutorials on 'survival skills', all above New York City. Despite the magnetic and electric shock defensive measures of her garments, her vision is not about cataclysm and isolation but how to live and survive *together* in a shared, if atmospherically altered, world. The other side of this architecture of air, however, is an exaggeration of isolation, and how the ultimate stability of the air is untenable – a mastery of the element tending to fall short.

'Worried about Climate Change? Don't Sweat It.' Perhaps one of the best and sardonic takes on corporate excess and climatic catastrophism is the Yes Men's Survivaball, a spoof product made in the name of the world's largest and most polluting corporations. The Survivaball inflatable is a personal solution to the environmental shocks predicted to result from climatic warming. We might see the Survivaball to be more than a joke,

Fuller's domes repeated at the Eden Project in Cornwall.

however, because, unfortunately, it exists at the ridiculous end of a continuum of what we might call 'dome' or 'insulating cultures' set against large-scale global atmospheric events. Survivaball takes individualism to the extreme. The Survivaball offers a perfectly sealed escape to the interior, although the head is curiously outside the ball. It is a defensible space to produce a rolling molecule-like being, which can generate its own electricity, move in water, fall from great heights, draw power from an animal, and temporarily accumulate with other Survivaballs! This 'aggregation' of balls comes with the possibility of dispensing with 'unneeded units when necessary'. In the world of the Survivaball, one chooses one's friends very carefully.[11]

'Keep it Slick: Infiltrating Capitalism with The Yes Men', curated by Astria Suparak, Miller Gallery at Carnegie Mellon University, 2008.

Back to Biosphere 2, and we learn again that even aerial isolation is imperfect because something is missing. The biome requires continual stabilization through its 'lungs'; structures that regulate air pressure and use massive cooling towers to exhaust the excess heat. Huge infrastructure is required to provide the capacity to watch, monitor and maintain the system and provide each inhabitant with four times their weight in oxygen each day. Yet the domes simply do not have the 'sublime irrationality, excess and absurdity of nature' Baudrillard bemoans. The engineers appear to have forgotten the things that give life life. In reality, even the biosphere's seal was never complete, insulation not quite absolute. From the outset, its climate and atmosphere failed. Carbon dioxide built up which killed off some animal species – notably honey bees, which slowed the pollination of plants. In the end, the air had to be 'scrubbed' to clean it of the dangerous surplus of CO_2, and even oxygen had to be pumped in. As usual air refused, preventing its ease into submission and simulation.

Perfect isolation

In 2012 the United Nations Headquarters in New York City underwent one of the first phases of a $1.9-billion refit and refurbishment. The Secretariat is the air-conditioned, 39-storey modernist skyscraper office building which stands on one side of the headquarters opposite the trapezoid Assembly, with its domed central meeting space inside. In shape, atmosphere and even in its exemption as an international zone inside the United State's sovereign territory, we might see the UN building as an almost perfect example of a giant kind of air bubble or volume, what E. B. White, following the Second World War, would call an 'island fantasy'.[12]

White, author of *Stuart Little* and *Charlotte's Web*, was not only calling the UN buildings an island fantasy either. Notwithstanding that Manhattan is an island, his comments are rather more attuned to the way New Yorkers lived, a population bestowed with the 'gift of loneliness and the gift of privacy'. It was a city, he argued, that was full of insulation. In fact, it was an insulator *par excellence*. And if it had a collective consciousness, it would be surprised that for the first time in its history, in the world of cold war threats and dome culture paranoia, it found itself 'destructible'. White was identifying New York as a potential 'target'. In an ever-resonant paragraph since the events of 9/11,

White explains how a 'single flight of planes no bigger than a wedge of geese can quickly end this island fantasy, burn the towers, crumble the bridges, turn the underground passages into lethal chambers, cremate the millions'.[13]

White's prose finds New York's insulating and defensive qualities to be one of its most valuable. Insulation is what holds the city together, a place made up of hundreds, millions of people, sharing almost the same space and the same air, little atmospheres insulated from one another by a degree of tolerance, ignorance and the 45 cm (18 in.) between White and an actor from *The Wizard of Oz* he finds himself sitting opposite on the subway. The key is this: New York is better than almost any other place at 'insulating the individual (if he wants it, and almost everybody wants or needs it)'.[14] But the gifts are contradictory. Insulation seems coupled with the possibility of participation. He writes of sitting in his hotel room in 90-degree heat, 'halfway down an air shaft in midtown. No air moves in or out of the room, yet I am curiously affected by emanations from the immediate surroundings.'[15] Unlike other cities, Manhattan enables the selective withdrawal from these events. As White explains,

> Since I have been sitting in this miasmic air shaft, a good many rather splashy events have been occurring in town. A man shot and killed his wife in a fit of jealousy. It caused no stir outside his block and only got a small mention in the papers. I did not attend. Since my arrival, the greatest air show ever staged in all the world took place in town. I didn't attend and neither did most of the other eight million other inhabitants, although they say there was quite a crowd. I didn't hear any planes except a couple of westbound commercial airliners that habitually use this air shaft to fly over . . . I heard the siren scream, but that was all there was to that – an eighteen-inch margin again. A man was killed by a falling cornice. I was not party to the tragedy, and again the inches counted heavily.[16]

The UN Secretariat.

The event, in other words, is optional and New York absorbs it. The UN Headquarters is just then another part of an accelerating race for insulation in an era of thermonuclear destruction and increasing migration and internationalism. The design is an attempt to overtake the 'spectral flight of planes'. The construction of the buildings is a 'carving out' of the institution, another 'interior city, to shelter, this time, all governments . . . a congress of visitors'.

The design team for the complex was understandably international and high profile. It also featured one of the most intricate and expensive ventilation systems in the world. The land by the East River and First Avenue had been bestowed to the UN by John D. Rockefeller, and was previously the site of slaughterhouses and other light industry. The decision to locate the UN in New York was made in London on 14 February 1946, with the actual plot purchase and the building costs not decided until the following year. The agreement between the United States and the General Assembly of the United Nations was signed on 26 June 1947, which gave the headquarters the mark of an international territory, outside the sovereign powers of the United States.[17]

The famous Swiss-born architect Le Corbusier was one of the ten-member panel of designers assisting Wallace K. Harrison, the director of planning appointed to the project. Like Biosphere 2, the massive concrete, glass, institutional and sovereign bubble of the United Nations Headquarters would come to rely upon an enormous air-conditioning and ventilation system to bring whatever climate its inhabitants wanted. This was particularly important given that 5,400 windows would line the curtain walls of the Secretariat building, made of a blue-green tinted Thermopane glass. This absorbing and self-reflecting surface meant that the buildings could really only be tolerable because of the ventilation system with some 4,000 individually controlled Carrier Weathermaster induction units beneath each window sill, and venetian blinds to provide some shade. The design had not come without conflict; Le Corbusier was adamant that the two glass facades of the building should hang *bris-soleil*, a form of shading that would stop the windows from transferring too much heat to the building, making working conditions unbearable. Le Corbusier even took his argument to the chair of the UN committee, arguing that it made little sense to build in New York 'where the climate is terrible in summer . . . I say this is dangerous, very seriously dangerous.'[18]

Le Corbusier's argument did not win out, but perhaps he had learned the hard way with his Cité de Refuge, a building completed in 1929 for the Salvation Army in Paris, which warmed – much like a greenhouse – to intolerable conditions for those within it. Indeed, while the principle behind the glass of the Secretariat was for transparency, Lewis Mumford complained that the tinted windows created the opposite effect. They bounced back any inward gaze, reflecting rather than disclosing the building's insides – a visual rebuttal to the penetration of public scrutiny.

The cartoonist Bernard 'Hap' Kliban satirized the construction of the Secretariat in 1950 with an image of two men – Pinch and Punch – watching the building of the project. A news item announces that the building will be equipped with 'individual air conditioning units to protect the health of workers recruited from widely different climatic and temperature zones'.[19] Studying the scene, Punch comments: 'I hear they can't even get together on the temperature they want in there . . .' To which Pinch replies, 'What's the difference – so long as they figure out some way to keep on working in the same building?'

Air as an environmental and political insulator was performed through the holy trinity of ventilation: 'holism, isolation and circulation'.[20] Yet the problems of the United Nations buildings share a longer genealogy with other political chambers such as the Capitol building in Washington, DC, and especially the debacle over the Houses of Parliament in nineteenth-century London. David Boswell Reid's design for the temporary Houses of Parliament sought to tackle a similar desire for insulation, although the conditions were quite different. Reid, primarily an engineer and expert in the principles of ventilation, was heavily

Air-conditioning the Capitol, Washington, DC, a Harris and Ewing photo taken in the 1930s.

involved in the redevelopment of the Houses following the fire of 1834, which had seriously damaged the existing buildings. He would also be employed as the 'ventilator' for Liverpool's magnificent St George's Hall in 1841.

Reid's principles are very interesting both for their metabolic rendering of the Parliament as a living organism with a head, lungs and body, and as a space of political atmospheres which had to be disciplined and maintained carefully by his system. His vision for the Houses was incredibly contradictory. It sought to separate the House from the stench of the neighbouring Thames by means of sucking the air in through high ventilation shafts or chimneys, planned initially to be built in the Victoria Tower and the Clock Tower of St Stephen's (now known as the Elizabeth Tower, housing the famous bell 'Big Ben'). This was to understand the Palace of Westminster as a body threatened by sickly airs. In order to isolate it sufficiently, it would need to not only suck in air, but essentially breathe filtered and carefully selected air as if Haldane's artificial respirator protected the workings of the lungs. The Houses of Parliament effectively gained respiratory organs to circulate air like an organism, fanning the political life of Parliament.

Reid's involvement in the buildings started much earlier as he was contracted by a select committee chaired by Sir Benjamin Hawes to consider the best mode of ventilating and warming the House. For Reid, the air of the outside becomes more than a potential danger to the chamber's members, since he saw atmosphere as a political medium. Seeing air 'in the same light as food', and finding the human at the bottom of 'the great aerial ocean', Reid naturally considered that each member of the House needed good aerial sustenance.[21] Under Reid's stewardship, air would be essential to the promulgation of the chamber's deliberating and decision-making, as the essential medium for politics was sound. The chamber was an 'ideal speech situation' or machine, as Paulo Tavares explains in more detail: 'air works as the medium that guarantees the voice of rhetoric and provides the adequate climate conditions for one to wait while listening to the others'.[22]

What followed was an incredible attention to detail in the complete mastery of the air of the chamber. The design of the House was considered by Reid as a pneumatic machine – an apparatus – that would and could immediately respond and adapt to the discomfort of the Parliament's members. Air could be adapted to the 'habits and feelings' of its inhabitants. Tiny holes were pierced into the flooring, 'a million apertures' which would pass through a carpet of hairs. Arrangements were made in the seating arrangements so that the air would not pass anywhere near a member's foot, preventing contamination from sweaty feet or other dirt and excrement that might have been collected on a walk through London![23] His principle was 'universal diffusion'. This meant that 'local currents may be entirely arrested and every space to have a like share of fresh air with the least possible movement'.[24]

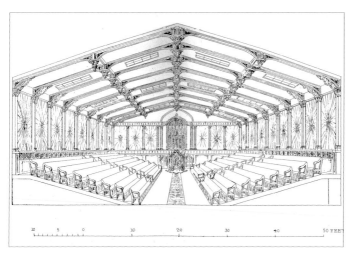

Drawings based on David Boswell-Reid's designs to ventilate the Houses of Parliament, 1835.

Reid's mastery of the airs of the House of Commons, 1834.

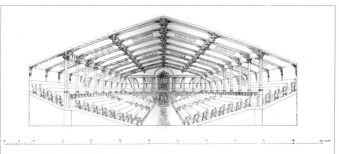

The air and acoustics of the House were examined as if a failing speech machinery that was disrupting political talk. Warm air currents were accused of refracting the sound passing from one side of the Commons to the other and rendering 'intonation indistinct', words 'congealing' like Mandeville's on 'northern air' a few centuries before. Sounds spilled in from the Old Palace Yard, coaches, cabs and omnibuses and, depending on the wind direction, indistinct noises could travel from one House to the other. In redesigning the shape, structure and air of the chamber, Reid's account almost rides on the pressure wave that diffuses the members' talk across the room and outwardly through the ventilation system.[25]

Reid's plan for the temporary House appears to have been well received. His air fulfilled its employment as political atmosphere almost to the tee. Lord Sudely would state in the House of Lords that they were indeed 'complete and perfect', while Sir Benjamin Hawes, who was Chairman of the Committee on Acoustics and Ventilation and founder of the Royal Humane Society, an organization we will explore later, told Reid 'You have facilitated public business, and prolonged the lives of public men.'[26] But things were not all rosy for Reid, his involvement in the new House would take a very different turn through his bitter disagreement with the architect Charles Barry, legal disputes and his eventual sacking from the project. Nor was his work on the temporary House without derision. In fact, the system that was eventually decided for the new House actually reversed Reid's design almost entirely from the system of isolation from the maladious airs of the Thames, towards a system more in line with expelling the dangerous airs that would accumulate within the building.

The main issue with Reid was his adherence to his own 'perfect' principles which could only ever be imperfectly practised. His measures of control seemed overstated, Reid, characterized by a popular London review as a pedant of air, a strict headmaster-like enforcer of air's discipline. The air was

> no longer 'the chartered libertine' of the olden times, but so watched and warded that any foul winds or exhalations found wandering about the streets will be arrested by a ventilating police, and confined to hard labour in certain penitentiary receptacles, when they will not be released 'till their *characters* shall be complete altered . . .
>
> Upside-down – inside-out – backwards or forwards – air bruising itself soft by falling upon other air – Dr Reid's universal system is ready for all emergencies, and can accommodate itself to all requirements, with no drawback or difficulty that may not be solved – and to Dr. Reid's own feelings most satisfactorily – by the formula before-mentioned, £. s. d.[27]

Reid had identified 34 kinds of air. The systematic parts of his book he divided into 'preface, introduction, index, and appendix'. Some 30 chapters, 857 paragraphs and 330 diagrams later, Reid was splitting airs and hairs; his work said to resemble a 'soufflé'!

Reid would come to settle in the United States, where his ideas were accepted with more enthusiasm, especially as ventilation became a direct instrument of population welfare, and not only for the political elite. Ventilation techniques like Reid's were being seen as the panacea to the population's respiratory diseases, a mechanism alongside the monitoring of dense tenements of cities such as New York and Chicago through new public health measures. On the back of Elisha Harris's work, and the penchant of reformers for new 'vital' statistical measures, the science of ventilation would prove much more 'concrete', to be employed on the wider scale of the city's urban climate.[28] It was a 'logical extension' of developments in other sanitation and building ventilation programmes. In Britain, Edwin Chadwick – the famous sanitation engineer – even projected a Pure Air Company with Dr Neil Arnott. They intended to 'aspirate' purer air from high above the city down into its streets and buildings.[29] This 're-engineering' of the atmospheric systems of cities could, through a complex arrangement of fans and chimneys, distribute fresh air through polluted streets.[30] But despite the widespread belief in ventilation, perhaps what unsettled Reid's critics most was that his obsessive and controlling measures over the atmosphere became even more of a nuisance than the air he sought to defend his inhabitants from.

The 'Invincible Fumigatory'

> He plunged the lighted end of his cigar into the powder, which began to smoke like a volcano, and send up fat, greasy wreaths of copper-colored smoke. In five seconds the room was filled with a most pungent and sickening stench – a reek that took fierce hold of the trap of your windpipe and shut it. The powder then hissed and fizzed, and sent out blue and

green sparks, and the smoke rose till you could neither see, nor breathe, nor gasp.[31]

In this scene in Simla, at 'Peterhoff', the viceregal lodge, the inhabitants of the house have already fled, coughing up the powder at the bottom of the stairs. The guards rushed in to investigate the disturbance while the ladies ran downstairs screaming 'fire'. The smoke continued to move, 'oozing out of the windows, and bellying along the verandahs, and wreathing and writhing', not one person could enter the house and the room where E. S. Mellish was demonstrating his new product, his 'Invincible Fumigatory'. At the foot of the stairs and bent double coughing, 'Glorious! Glorious!', sobbed the viceroy with laughter. 'Not a germ, as you justly observe, could exist! I can swear it. A magnificent success!'

In Kipling's world published in *Plain Tales from the Hills* of the colonial hill station at Simla (now Shimla), the air is another island atmosphere. In this story about a germ scientist demonstrating his invention to the viceroy, the irony is that the removal of maladious germs from the hill station air only replaces it with another nuisance. The powder gone airborne makes the rooms of the mansion house entirely uninhabitable and would not be endured for long. Yet it was the same desire to keep apart from air – germs by smoke in the scientist's demonstration – that underpinned the hill station's purpose within Britain's wider colonial project. This was the atmospheric detachment of the administration of the British Raj from the rest of India's air and its people.

The British officials could not stomach the Indian summers.[32] In the lowlands, on the coast and on the plains, the air and the heat, the dust and the din, all took their toll. The colonials nostalgically longed for home. They created a little piece of it in the higher and cooler climates of the mountains. The Madras government had the Nilgiri, in Bengal it was Darjeeling, and Burma the town of Maymyo (Pyin Oo Lwin). These hill stations were the homes of the Raj's summer administration and the retreats of India's elites. Later, they would provide the summer vacation spots for the country's emerging middle classes. During the rest of the year, India's administrators yearned for the high ground, and the comforts of blankets, log fires and smells, 'whiffs of sawn wood from the carpenters' shops, of the intoxicating scent of resinous pine needles trodden on a picnic on a sunny afternoon'.[33]

Hill stations such as Darjeeling and the Ootacamund came coupled with the administrative measures that sought to study and govern the nature of population, refigured as atmospheric subjects. The hill stations were places primarily for health, recuperation and leisure, built with home-like qualities reconstructing the English country estate. They were 'cool, green, and unpopulated. The contrast with the lowlands seemed to provoke the question, "could this be India?"'[34] In the case of Ootacamund, assessments ranging from Tennyson's description of the 'sweet half-English air' to a later paean to its value as 'an island of British atmosphere hung above the Indian plains' communicated the site's granting of permissive escape.[35] The climate of the 'Other' is reinscribed with the characteristics of the safe and the familiar – Lord Lytton describing the summer capital of the Madras presidency thus: 'I affirm it to be a paradise. The afternoon was rainy and the road muddy but such beautiful English rain, such delicious English mud.'[36]

'Snooty Ooty' was perhaps the highest expression of those atmospheres reserved for India's administrators, founded by a place to take 'the air on Simla's Mall'. The stations were communities of leisure and gossip, the sites of high jinks, tennis matches and fancy-dress balls. Unsurprisingly, there was much talk of the 'grave scandal' or 'dereliction of duty' at this exodus. It was a sense of government perceived 'above the reach of human censure, not to say human observation, amid the cloud-capped mountains and mirth-bearing breezes of Simla', which fostered the sentiment of an ever-growing detachment between the colonizers and the colonized.

Indian air, however, was not such a problem for everyone. The analysis of women's diaries explores the drab world many migrants would encounter on their return to England, air separating their two existences into two demarcated spheres of air.

The Viceregal Lodge
at Simla.

'Indian life which was our real life', Vera Birdwood explains, while
'the strange almost dehumanized periods of leave in England
where we enjoyed ourselves and breathed the good English air',
were something quite boring.[37] On these return visits, home and
away are contrasted through air. Iris Portal remembers how she
'stood in the window of the dining room of that tall, dark house
and looked out at rain falling and wondered why there was no
colour anywhere'; 'this air felt leaden or lifeless, I don't mean so
much climatically [but] as in atmosphere', she explained.[38]

Even the journeys to the hill stations were stories of encap-
sulation and middle-class comfort to be repeated in modern

India, seeking the escape in ways similar to their colonial counterparts. Anita Desai, raconteur of India's middle classes, remembers now with some relish the inconveniences and minor discomforts of the bumps, jolts and shocks of the railway journey up into the mountains. She could almost be ghosting Kipling. Packing her belongings, with 'travel fever rising in our throats till we felt sick', Anita and her siblings make their way through 'the greasy, stifling bazaars whose entire population seemed to be stretched out on the pavements for air' on their way to the old railway station.[39] She remembers the electric fans, buzzing like flies against the ceiling and notably, 'before there was air-conditioning that brought with it not only cool air but protection from soot and grime so that clean bed linen, curtains and carpeting became possible'. By 1939, the Simla Municipal Committee had noticed the demographics of visitors to be increasingly made up of doctors, school, teachers, students, landlords and businessmen.

C. B. Young,
Nainital, Kumaon,
N. W. Provinces, India,
1874, oil on canvas.

Air's nuisances, however, are no longer expressed in the exile of India's government to the hills or its middle classes seeking relief. We might see that the new hill stations of India and our urbanizing planet are in fact to be found in the city, where extravagant and self-sufficient high-rise blocks such as 'Antilla' illustrate a cocooning away of the super-rich from the polluted air which is estimated to be the fifth-largest killer in the country. At the same time, an urban bourgeois community has come to legitimize in law what are effectively large-scale population evictions and displacement because of local atmospheric discomfort and nuisance.[40]

Things came to a head in Delhi in 2000 through the removal of 98,000 small-scale and 'polluting' industrial units, in an advancement of an environmentalist agenda of aesthetic and social purification. Following the closures of the small-scale polluters, severe riots and social unrest erupted as Delhi's urban slums were identified as the birthplace of the city's environmental and

Government House, Ootacamund, 1909.

social problems. Oozing liquids, fecal matter, informal industrial pollutants and household waste constitute the unsanitary threat to social order and aesthetic sensibility of the rising urban middle classes. Mills, 'smokestack industries' and effluent-producing manufacturing were to be 'tucked away out of sight'. Workers were made to live well away from the eyes, ears and noses of the well-to-do. Delhi has since embarked on a decade-long period of slum clearance and contraction, and the removal and criminalization of the slum population by the new definition of a nuisance. In this evolving legal category, the dwellings that make up the slums become inseparable from their status as social bother. Moreover, the inhabitants of these dwellings are divorced from any categorization as reasonable citizens with rights over public land because only 'unreasonable' people are believed to live and pollute in this way.

There are other experiences of slum air that must be accounted for. Telling a different side to this story from those very dwellers who are accused of being the nuisance, we find that this is a way of life that is very difficult to change. Informal and insufficient sanitation infrastructures in Rafinagar, Mumbai, provoke disgust especially amongst those very dwellers forced to live in such circumstances. Research shows how open defecation is sometimes the only option given the inadequate provision of toilets, forcing private acts into open spaces, by roads and gardens and wastelands near communal toilet blocks.[41] Narratives of escape from these atmospheres are common. For example, Danny Boyle's film *Slumdog Millionaire* (2008) gives one arc of the boy Jamal, who is transported from a slum to the heights of Mumbai's skyscrapers, where, with Salim, he contemplates the view; taking in the clear air they point out the site of their former home.[42]

The air is the enemy

Artistic and political movements may have easily predicted the failure of the insulating impetus, and gone some lengths to attempt to subvert or send it up. The 'Destruction of RSG-6' opened at the Galleri Exi in Odense, Denmark, on 22 June

'Antilla', Mumbai.

1963. The exhibition was placed in the basement, and for good reason. Designed and inspired by the Situationist International arm in Denmark, the exhibit was based on a regional government fallout shelter which had been found outside Reading, Berkshire, by a group of activists. The shelters' 'condensed subterranean version' was a sign for society's 'pathological excess', its lack of societal health. Their prognosis was a world of shelters, acknowledged 'as an air conditioned vale of tears'. The Dutch arm of the Situationists sought to continue the exposure of Britain's nuclear shelter policy by reproducing its air. Their intention was to engender an expressive outcome of shock by simulating the shelter, just differently. It would have the same 'atmosphere', but with a 'thought-provoking ambiance'. The first room of the gallery had sirens, stretchers and dead bodies. In the second, pictures of politicians were placed on the walls and the audience was told to fire at them with a rifle, winning a free copy of the catalogue should they hit the eye of a politician. Guy Debord even suggested that the light should be 'soft and disagreeable', and that 'The air is rendered difficult to breathe by an excess of deodorant. Two assistants dressed in anti-nuclear jumpsuits (cowls, goggles) oblige the people to remain 10 minutes in this space.'

The American urban critic Lewis Mumford describes Leo Tolstoy's satire of modern man 'sealing up the windows of his house and mechanically exhausting the air, so that he might, by utilizing a still more extravagant mechanical apparatus, pump air back again – instead of merely opening the window'.[43] Tolstoy could not possibly have believed that his vision would actually come true, deployed not for the contagious and bad airs of the unventilated city, but as a common technique by architects and designers of private homes and public buildings, even 'in the midst of the open country'. Mumford's cartoon for the magazine *Survey* in 1925 captures some of this madness. It contains a sketch reminiscent of Hugh Ferriss's anticipatory drawing of New York the year before. Mumford's two tiny characters stand on the top of a building looking up at an even larger New York skyline. 'Yes sir,' says one of the characters, 'that's the city of the future! Two-hundred storey skyscrapers! Air pumped in from the country. Every cubic foot of space used day and night. Mechanically perfect!' The other exclaims, 'Magnificent! Will any one live there?'[44]

5 Mirage

> At length he paused: a black mass in the gloom,
> A tower that merged into the heavy sky;
> Around, the huddled stones of grave and tomb:
> Some old God's-acre now corruption's sty:
> He murmured to himself with dull despair,
> Here Faith died, poisoned by this charnel air.[1]

Air is nightmarish in the poisonous 'charnel air' of James Thomson's poem *The City of Dreadful Night* (1880). It holds things and people down under its thick canopy. Sanity and even time are held in suspension. Life is almost unlivable.

In the zone of half-awake, we witness the strange bending and warping of time and space as we drift in and out of a restless night of busy thoughts, imaginations and hallucinations. Air is disturbing. The night air too warm and close, hot, we wake in a sweat and lie frustrated. Thomson's poem tells of the melancholy atmospheres of a walker forced into the night in search of distraction from their weary self. His efforts of acquiescence are tiring and exhausting. The world is experienced by the insomniac as a blue-grey sort of scene. He exists in a time that seems to stretch on just short of dawn – a bleached or monochromatic sort of time as if the colour had been washed out. The world is stripped of its vibrancy. Things decay and rot whilst the walker trudges on in thought and through gloom. The air suspends a depressed psyche wrought by fatigue and the longing for submission to dreams, to the fall of sleep. The realization that morning is coming envelopes the world into despair and solemnity. Day comes too soon.

Yale geography professor and environmental determinist Ellsworth Huntington saw something lurking in the climate, something that was determining higher rates of insanity and mental health problems. He had published *Civilization and Climate* in 1915, arguing for a much broader place for the climate within the advances of human societies, and thereby echoing Hippocrates in many ways. The weather, he argued, could be compared to the manner a driver might treat their horse. The worst, he supposed, would be a climate most similar to a driver who might 'whip their horses and urge them to the limit all the time. They make rapid progress for a while, but in the end they exhaust their animals.'[2] This would resemble a type of climate that was 'always stimulating' and where 'nervous exhaustion is likely to prevail and insanity becomes common'. The best would be a type that 'may whip his horse sometimes and sometimes let him walk, but what he does chiefly is to urge the animal gently with the voice, then check him a little with the rein'. This urging and checking helps to conserve the animal's strength. An analogous climate might have enough variety to be stimulating, but without the exhaustion or nervous tension.

Seeing suicide as a symptom of mentally sapping climatic conditions, Huntingdon would correlate u.s. suicide rates with the weather across the states. The worst cases to be found in regions where excesses of temperature changes prevail. Californians, he argued, were as if 'horses which are urged to the limit so that some of them become unduly tired and breakdown'.[3] The too 'uniformly stimulating' atmospheres of fogs blowing in from the sea, succeeded by bright, warm weather, argues Huntington, may account for California having the highest rate of suicide in the United States. In 1922 this equalled, per 100,000 people, 47.8 people in San Diego, 37.9 in Sacramento and 30.4 in San Francisco. Set against fifteen people in the eastern cities, this marked a notable difference.

Although his work is considered today as both determinist and reductionist, it was influential. Huntington would explore places and technologies that could tame the divergences from the ideal comforting type in his work for the Atmosphere and Man Committee which he chaired in 1922. The committee was a group of influential North American scientists, industrialists and policymakers, who would shape the widespread emergence of the new technology of the air conditioning unit, especially in America's South, albeit without much acknowledgement of the environmental consequences.[4] The air-conditioning units we saw in the previous chapter owe their invention to Willis Haviland Carrier. Carrier had been granted a patent in 1906 for his Apparatus for Treating Air. This was the first of a series of patents which would bring the 'control of air' into the domain of professional engineers, and enable internal environments to be regularly cooled and (de)humidified. Joining forces to form the Carrier Engineering Corporation in 1915, the progress of air conditioning would be slow and eventually found sustained popularity in the interwar movie theatre and the department store, such as Chicago's 'Hudson's' in 1926.

The air conditioner would create isolated pockets of cool air on a massive scale to produce 'comfort' to appeal to particular bodily and cultural sensibilities of air. It is perhaps through those pockets that we might explore the principles of air's insulation and its detrimental effects on a more intimate, psychological level.

Oasis

The air seems to ripple, trembling in the heat which looks more like vapour. Some sort of shape seems to be there. It looks as if it is getting larger, like a tower moving irresistibly closer. The shape turns into a horse with a rider. Lawrence's guide runs to fetch a gun. Crack! The Bedouin sherif Ali has shot the guide from an inconceivable distance with his rifle. This is the 'whack in the guts' that David Lean sought to stir in the audience in the classic scene from his epic *Lawrence of Arabia* (1962), where T. E. Lawrence meets Ali for the first time. This is also one of the most celebrated arrivals in cinema. The mirage is not exceptional to Lawrence, neither is it an uncommon trope in both colonial and Islamic literature – *saraab* is Arabic for 'mirage'. Lawrence had tried to capture the mirage on his own film. His diaries record the date, Monday 17 July 1911, 'Much mirage: tried to photograph one pool, but failed: nothing showed up on the ground-glass.' The mirage distorts a tower at Harran (in Anatolia, Turkey), which is made 'elongated' as he travels towards it. The tower 'becked and bobbed in the most fantastic way, now shivering from top to bottom, now bowing to the right or left, now a deep curtsey forwards'.[5] Instead, in Lean's *Lawrence* the mirage is first the mesmerizing boredom of the desert landscape, before it becomes a threat, a bubble of contemplation burst by the shock of the shot.

The desert mirage expresses the 'fantastic' and the fanciful in the Arabian environment. Robert Southey's *Thalaba the Destroyer* would exemplify these sorts of texts. Published in 1801, *Thalaba* is a fanciful tale of sorcery, where the 'hot air quivers, and the sultry mist Floats o'er the desert'.[6] Southey and other writers would borrow heavily from the descriptions of the Middle East found in sources such as *Shaw's Travels*, where the phenomenon was likened to a 'collection of water'. The morphology of the mirage shimmers with a colonial ache for what it cannot quite posses. It is always retreating. A quivering motion of the desert's breath, the mirage is a false appearance.

A mirage is in fact caused by differences in air temperature bending light. What Lawrence was really seeing was the desert reflecting the sky because the light photons take the quickest path possible caused by the excessively hot desert sands heating up the air above them. In other words, the desert reflects the sky

Mirage.

because the light is taking a curved path, not a straight one. The air can enable things to appear where they ordinarily would not be, and that is a theme worth following.

The historian of the American South Robert Arsenault has explored the integral role of the air conditioner in radically re-shaping the air of public buildings, workplaces and homes, even the human geography of the United States. By 1960, 20 per cent of homes in the South owned an air conditioner, by 1973 80 per cent of cars had air conditioning, as it became felt as an almost legal right. However, this also contributed to a massive shift in population density which almost doubled from between 1930 to 1980 due to declining mortality, and, interestingly, new routines of travel and migration to the 'sun belt'. The 1970 census was dubbed the 'air conditioned census' by the *New York Times* because it captured the evolving effect of the technology in creating attractive and comfortable climates in the South, even in the summer. Sydney F. Markham's *Climate and Energy of Nations* (1942) would help to identify a new symbolic border, pushing beyond the Mason–Dixon line that divided the nation. An 'axis of culture' seemed to be possible from the climate and the air; an effective frontier to limit national progress.

Since the discovery of oil in 1966, Dubai, the emirate on the southeast of the Persian Gulf, is a newer sort of desert mirage. It is now a global hub of financial services, real estate and tourism. A material shock, arguably like Ali's rifle shot, in the 120-degree heat of the Arabian Peninsula, Dubai is a weird hypermodern spectacle of consumer capitalism. It is what the urban scholar Mike Davis has described as a 'an eerie chimera ... a hallucin-atory pastiche of the big, the bad and the ugly'. Islands, gated communities and gigantic monolithic structures such as the Burj Khalifa tower completed in 2010 – a half-empty $4.1-billion building that is arguably more suitable for film shoots – popu-late this place. Dubai is incredibly well represented by the air-conditioned and cooled climatic biospheres of luxury it has created in the hostile desert climate. This has not stopped swimming pools, shopping malls and indoor ski slopes popping up. Dubai is a place only possible because of the management

Ski Dubai.

of its air, conditioned to cool the occupants of its theme-park environment, a place likely to dissolve back into the sands of the desert once its economy has run dry of oil, its exploited migrant labour returned, and its visitors reduced to a trickle.

Echoing this agora of air-conditioned consumption spaces are the strange islands of military bases dotted around the Middle East. Elsewhere in the Persian Gulf, u.s. and other international forces are to be found stationed in places like Kandahar in Afghanistan. For air-conditioning expert Stan Cox, there is an irony and madness in the movement or displacement of militarized air to these contexts – vast environments of cooled air brought to the most unlikely places. And they are permissible only because of the liquidity of oil. According to Cox, roughly 85 per cent of the fuel hauled to Iraq and Afghanistan in 2008 was being used for air conditioning. Are these just another mirage in the desert, mirages made by the Dunkin Donuts and Burger Kings; sports centres, department stores, Pizza Huts, Starbucks, Baskin-Robbins ice cream and miniature golf courses, football fields, Hertz car hire, internet cafés and swimming pools? These are tiny cities with the facilities of anywhere in the United States, yet with the same air.[7] As Cox explores in more detail, the air of these bases brings America to the desert, the smell of pizzas reminding the soldiers of home.[8]

These small islands of pseudo-imperial and atmospheric sovereignty are not new to the Middle East. The year 2011 saw u.s. forces hopping by helicopter from the border of Afghanistan into Abbottabad, Pakistan, on their mission to capture or kill Osama bin Laden. Their extraterritorial assassination of the al-Qaeda figurehead strangely reproduced another and much earlier colonial pocket. Abbottabad took its name from Major James Abbott, who became deputy commissioner of the region in 1849, a popular hill station for the British seeking cooler climates from the plains, which he left in 1853.[9] The town became a military

A Pizza Hut franchise at Camp Bastion, 2010.

cantonment, stationing the British Gurkha force, and the muse for his dreadful poem which starts, 'I remember the day when I first came here. And smelt the sweet Abbottabad air.'

Madness

For Aravind Adiga's main protagonist, Balram, in *The White Tiger* (2008), the sealed air-conditioned car Balram drives through Delhi exemplifies the escape of the middle classes from the country's problems and its poor. City air is routinely filtered, face masks adorn much of the populace who attempt to avoid the pollutants. It is so bad, he explains, 'that is takes ten years off a man's life'.[10] This is not air for all. Balram's employers avoid it. Balram does too, 'it is just nice, cool, clean, air-conditioned air for us'. The air-conditioned apartment, but especially the car, appear to stand for modern India. The many automobiles seem to Balram to resemble dark eggs, painted spheres with tinted windows, bustling around the streets of Delhi. The closed and air-conditioned chambers he describes could be São Paulo, Beijing, Lagos or Mexico City, which have seen car use skyrocket. Or, rather, they resemble accounts of the incredible congestion and air pollution of many megacities that populate the global south, causing vast respiratory problems for the inhabitants of the cities' dense and sprawling form, and regular evacuations as air quality indicators advise and visibility is reduced to 100 metres. Even Beijing has recently dropped its 'blue sky' days, to recognize more comprehensive air quality measures because its air pollution appears to be worsening and going 'beyond index'. This followed geopolitical disputes over the u.s. embassy's air pollution readings for Beijing, which conflicted with the official Chinese government data.

In Adiga's narrative of Delhi, the conditioned and comfortable car is a condition for ignorance, shielding its occupants from the atmospheric woes. Occasionally, these eggs open a crack. Out of the egg stretches 'a woman's hand, dazzling with gold bangles. It does not stay for long as the window goes up, and the egg is released.'[11]

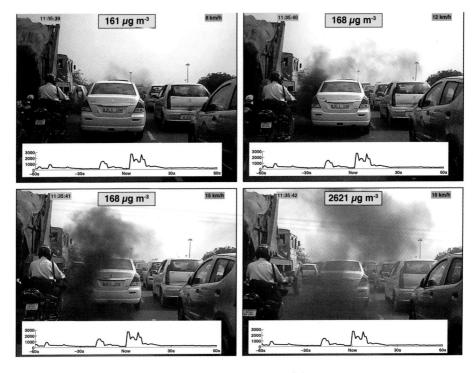

Air particulate concentrations on Delhi's roads.

Perhaps the car articulates the fragmented lives of the megacity. The controlled climate is protection from the fumes and wisps of exhausts,[12] the fog of petrol and tobacco which hides a bureaucracy corrupted by bought officials, a murky world of half-light within which 'multitudes of small, thin, grimy people' live. 'We were like separate cities', Balram explains, 'inside and outside the dark egg'. Maybe the Mahindra & Mahindra Corporation's desirable four-wheel drive Bolero is the extreme of Balram's commentary. This car is all about muscularity and presence. Or Tata's Nano is more apt as it almost is a tiny egg, the small shell selling for less than $2,000. They both illustrate the tendency towards the appropriation of the road and public space with a personalized fortified air. Tinted windows and sealed-up spaces even signal social status. But perhaps the reason Balram murders his employer outside the car as he checks the wheel is because the internal space of the egg, its plastic fittings, nylon seat cushions and its air, have become so desirable that they are sacred. The tyre iron is his weapon of choice as he smashes in his master's skull.

Maladious hot air might have been seen as an agitator of the passions, provoking a hot temper, yet the tipping point for Balram's murderous decision is in fact unequal air. Perhaps Balram's city is India's answer to 1980s Manhattan, which would set the scene for the ludicrous heights of the financial services, the ultra-excesses of consumer capital and the indifferent lives of the super-rich yuppies, who inhabit the world of air-conditioned apartments and office buildings. These are the new 'atmospheric natures' of manufactured air in the city, as David Gissen has christened this world, which has arisen dramatically since the 1960s. The cleaned, dry air of the air conditioning unit taunts Bret Easton Ellis's deranged psychopathic and New York banker, Patrick Bateman, in his novel *American Psycho* (1991). Bateman is an evil but somehow sympathetic figure in the business of 'murders and executions' (not mergers and acquisitions). In amongst Bateman's multiple-page diatribes on Huey Lewis and the News, Genesis and other '80s music icons, is a real sense of distance in a society all but vacated of levity and responsibility. Possibly the most poignant and pathetic scene happens when Bateman creeps into the men's toilets at the Yale Club to strangle Luis Carruthers.

> In slow motion, my own heavy breathing blocking out all other sounds, my vision blurring slightly around the edges, my hands move up over the collar of his cashmere blazer and cotton-flannel shirt, circling his neck until my thumbs meet at the nape and my index fingers touch each other just above Luis's Adam's apple.[13]

Luis has mistaken Patrick's attempt at murder for an act of love. Patrick is paralysed. He is choked. He tries to squeeze the breath out of Luis with even more force, imagines his trachea squashed and crumbling, but it is his own air which falters. The 'soap bubble' world of lofty separation from below, encapsulating boxes of apartments and elevators – 'temporary castles in the air' – are broken in this moment of touch in the space of a toilet cubicle. All barriers broken, Bateman can neither murder nor breathe.

Bateman is perhaps the amplification of figures seen in works such as Tom Wolfe's *Bonfire of the Vanities* (1987) and the kind of vertical and air-conditioned society Jonathan Raban would call Manhattan's 'Air People' in his *Hunting Mister Heartbreak* (1991). Written and published within a few years of one another, *Bonfire*, *Psycho* and *Hunting* are stunning critiques of air of a certain kind. The 'Air People' are the society of identikit Wall Street workers who inhabit an ethereal but monotonous vertical world, taking E. B. White's notion of insulated and ventilated urbanity to its ultimate end. Rather than ride the subways that brought White side-by-side with a famous actor, atmospheric insulation is the organizing principle for Wolfe's Sherman.[14] 'That was the ticket', 'insulation', Sherman learns; 'you've got to insulate, insulate, insulate', his father tells him.[15] This is a defensible life lived at high altitude, where the old Manhattan of streets and squares is defended by secessional security and surveillance systems, each inhabitant 'a balloonist floating high over the lawless wreckage of the city'.[16]

As Bateman daydreams murderous fantasies, Raban finds it impossible to find sense in the Park Avenue apartments utterly divorced from the ground below. Raban's inner thoughts come dangerously close to Bateman's, but murder is not what he has in mind. Rather, he is responding to recent news reports, and, like Bateman, no one else seems to notice. The literal vertical existence of this new financial and social elite supports their insulation from the matters of real life which are moving maddeningly further apart, becoming less and less held together by the 'umbilical of the elevators':

> Up here we're sailing through the sky where the air is keen and the view is of a flawless sweep of luminous indigo blue. You're way below the cloud-ceiling. You're not even a dot to us, *buddy*.[17]

The apparent atmosphere of protection or perhaps even refuge seen in these novels apes the conditioning of city life in an increasing number of Manhattan's spaces to be climatically controlled for the purpose of preserving priceless objects and cultural artefacts. Gissen examines the Dendur Temple, moved from the banks of the Nile to the Metropolitan Museum of Art's remarkable purpose-built, hydrographically controlled building in 1978. The air of these inner spaces is a protection from the turbulence and pollution of outside. The American Psycho also perceives the outside to be unwholesome, full of decay, putrid atmospheres oozing from the bodies on the pavements. The wind that shoots up and down the city's canyons of concrete and stone smells of burning chestnuts mingling with car exhaust fumes. He realizes that there is nothing inside him. There is only order, a perfection that he seeks to reproduce outwardly in his multiple fitness, health and facial routines, and immaculate taste in the Air People's uniform of Polo sweaters, Valentino suits and other designer labels. He is a vacuum – a crater – the desert his landscape of purity and abstraction. In *Bonfire*, Sherman's story has an Icarian arc. His fall sees his personal 'cavity' entered as his misdemeanours go public. He can keep out the inquiring public no longer. Death is the only option he contemplates to rid himself of these intruders, 'he could keep them out only in the same manner that he could deny air to his lungs once and for all'.[18]

Torture, or the air in a state of war with me

Bateman's maddening air does not seem to be unique, but much of this appears to concern a certain sharing or intimacy of air a little different to its miasmic and humoural association. In Nietzsche's admission, air speaks of something of the Other, which he has to endure. He cannot help but detect, '*smell* – the proximity or (what am I saying?) the innermost aspect, the "innards" of every soul'.[19] Like Bateman and Grenouille (who did not smell), it is then only solitude that can relinquish their revulsion, 'a return to myself, the breath of free, light, playful air ... to solitude ... to *purity*'.[20]

In the relation of atmosphere to madness there never seems enough air for two, especially within the circumstances of war. On the scarred battlefields of the Western Front during the First World War, Erich Maria Remarque's classic novel *All Quiet on the Western Front* (1929) tells of Paul – a German soldier heading into Russia – who shelters from the shells and machine-gun fire inside a crater. He is about to leave when a body, which he assumes to be an enemy soldier, falls on top of him. Prepared with a knife, in wild madness he stabs frantically at the body until it 'goes limp and collapses'. Paul's hand is sticky with blood and mud.

The air of the trenches in this story is suffocating, but not only with the gas that Haldane was exploring. Waiting with the 'other man', it is his breathing that drives Paul to insanity. The gurgling starts. Is it from his stab-marked chest or throat? It sounds to Paul 'as if he is roaring, every breath is like a scream, like thunder'.[21] Paul crawls away to a corner of the hole and sits watching him, his eyes fixed on him. The gurgling continues; the air is all that is left of the solider. 'He's dead', Paul tells himself, 'he can't feel anything any more; that gurgling, it can only be the body.' Paul tries to bandage and compress the man's wounds, feeling terrible sympathy for the first man he has killed in hand-to-hand combat. Maybe it is not madness, but the waiting almost does it, it gives the other man a power over him as if an 'invisible dagger'. The gurgling starts back up again and by twilight 'reason evaporates', 'every gasp strips my heart bare'. By the afternoon, he is dead. Respite. Paul may 'breathe again', but he soon wishes for the gurgling 'in fits and starts, hoarse, sometimes a soft whistling noise and then hoarse and loud again'.[22]

If air can be tortuous, is it surprising that our manufactured weathers have been turned against us? In the history of war, the air conditioner's cooling has become a routine technology of torture, playing a significant role in techniques intended to solicit confessions and (supposedly) valuable information from captured prisoners, insurgents and detainees. 'Cold Cell' is one of several known CIA techniques that involves immersing the subject in cold air, normally projected from fans or an air conditioning unit. For one prisoner, detained within counter-terrorism practices under the 'war on terror', this put 'the air in a state of war with me'.[23] This kind of 'environmental manipulation' by air is even commonplace in torture manuals and a central part of the u.s. Army's Survival Evasion Resistance and Escape (SERE) training, methods which have been systematically 'flipped' onto detainees.

Hypothermia seems to be a common outcome of the abusive use of the air conditioner and bears strong historical parallels to the hypothermic medical testing conducted by the Nazis at concentration camps such as Dachau, even though their purpose was quite different. Prisoners who were sent to the Russian Gulag would even use climate as a way of distributing punishment.[24] For example, the use of temperature as torture can be seen in Aleksandr Solzhenitsyn's *The Gulag Archipelago* (1938). Following the invasion and occupation of Iraq, in Camp Nama on the outskirts of Baghdad International Airport, u.s. Special Access Program (SAP) personnel were accused of repeatedly stripping detainees naked, spraying them with cold water and then seating them next to air conditioners. Emails gathered from the FBI's visits to Guantanamo Bay show not only examples of air cooling, but the use of excessively hot air too. On one occasion, an officer reports that the air conditioning has been turned off, making the room temperature excessively hot. The detainee was so distressed it appears that they began pulling their own hair out.[25] Suffocatingly hot air is also commonplace in examples of torture and prisoner mistreatment. Born in the colonial wars of South Asia, the 'sweat box' was sometimes made of metal and held in the sun to create intolerably warm microclimates of discomfort.

The enrolment of air into these techniques has even seen it used to kill as hot air and a lack of air have been deployed in examples of prisoner mistreatment that suspend human rights, the laws of war and any trace of human dignity. The artist Milica Tomić's project *CONTAINER* recreates the scene of a crime based on a 2001 mass grave discovered in Afghanistan from the early stages of the Afghanistan War.[26] Physicians for Human Rights spearheaded the campaign providing evidence that some 2,000 Taliban and al-Qaeda prisoners were held by an Afghan warlord near Sherberghan. The prisoners are reported to have been suffocated in container trucks and cargo containers which were left in the heat of the desert. Ventilating the containers was another act of murder. As the container's inhabitants began to beg for air, clawing at the skins of their neighbours, licking perspiration and even drinking the blood from open wounds, the Northern Alliance soldiers fired at the containers in order to allow the air in. As they did so, of course, life came spilling out. U.S./UN forces may have attempted to cover up the atrocity and satellite evidence has located several mass graves where the bodies were subsequently deposited, but questions are still being asked of the role of U.S./Allied troops in supporting and overseeing the Afghani warlord.

Monotony

According to Huntington, the 'monotony' of air and climate 'deadens'. Too much of the same air may give rise to the kinds of weaknesses we have seen in the 'orientalist' readings of air and climate that located these qualities in the tropics. It was believed that high and consistent humidity and temperatures could cause 'drunkenness, immorality, anger, and laziness'. The tropics and even colonial outposts in the Caribbean – as William Hillary would write on Barbados in 1766 for instance – were places of disease and debauchery, since they were on the edge of civility and so far away from home.[27] Something similar seems to be true of the air conditioner. Robert Arsenault's criticism of the transformation of the American South by cooling is its ultimate erasure of different kinds of air and the different sorts of cultures that go with it.[28] The air conditioner removed the South's rhythms of heat during the long hot summer to the extent that 'the South is not the South', explains Arsenault. There is no need for the porch to take shade under, no reason to nap in the afternoon, the temperature is homogenized by a landscape of shopping malls and interiority.

Milica Tomić,
CONTAINER, 2010.

Air conditioning takes the place of our own bodily systems of regulating our temperature through perspiration, as well as more traditional and less energy-guzzling techniques. These include passive cooling and natural ventilation techniques which have been used for hundreds of years and are commonly found in Persian architecture, such as the *Badgir* in Iran. The city of Yazd, famous for its octagonal wind catcher at Dolat Abad, is known as *šahr-e bādgīrhā*, the city of wind catchers. Even in Dubai, a *Badgir* can be found just a few miles from the city.

To what extent then, might we be able to adapt to excessively cold or hot airs? Might we have different levels of comfort and expectations of air? The architect Lisa Heschong's classic book *Thermal Delight* (1979), was one of the first treatises to ask these kinds of questions.[29] Perhaps part of the problem is that the

standards used for the conditioning of air have not accounted   A *Badgir* at Yazd.
for these differences and capacities to adapt to climate all that
well, or that we might actually like some diversity in temperature
to be found, for example, in the sauna, or the enjoyment of coming in from the cold. Having said that, the massive growth of the
Chinese and Indian high-rises seems to value the homogeneity
of Western building types, propagated in the dominant international standards as set by the American Society of Heating,
Refrigerating and Air-Conditioning Engineers (ASHRAE) which
was founded in 1894.[30] These standards of so-called comfort
have a history, originating in the studies of factory workers we
saw earlier, and pioneered in the identification of 'thermal comfort zones' by T. Bedford at the London School of Hygiene and
Tropical Medicine in the 1930s, and later Ole Fanger's 'heat
balance' model. Thermal comfort zones would set standards,
particularly for modern office design, by helping to stimulate

productivity, as seen in the Seagram building in New York designed by Mies van der Rohe in the International Style in 1958, while Lloyd's of London's new air-conditioned underwriting room began construction in 1952 to seat almost 1250 persons.

> The underwriters in the Room
> Have found their comfort such a boon,
> Their metabolic rates are gauged
> By subtle and unusual ways.

In an air-conditioned world, the process of bodily cooling by the evaporation of sweat from the skin (latent energy transforming into the evaporated vapour) is replaced by the artificial climates of the home, workplace and public space. This might make some of us so used to these airs that we cannot bear to live anywhere else, nor can we stand the sensations of our own natural bodily cooling. In this new culture of cool, the adage 'Horses sweat, men perspire and women glow' is now increasingly unlikely as we simply do not tolerate sweat as we used to. The result is a form of social ordering that 'strips us human animals of odour and dampness'.[31] Research on Singapore's youth shows that bodily perspiration may even be seen as a form of pollution.[32] Like the association of air with smell discussed earlier, sweat is simply 'out of place' on the body in today's culture.

According to the technical research, the dominant norms of comfort in many places do not reflect their 'climatic and cultural context'. India's new buildings follow the ASHRAE standard, setting air conditioning at levels that accounted for 46 per cent of India's final energy use between 1995 and 2005. Studies of thermal comfort have shown that the comfort expectations of populations between temperate, cold climate and hot tropical climates are quite different. We might ask how air conditioning in fact *conditions*, creating monotonous environments of its own. As we saw in the South, air conditioning creates similar uses in energy production, habits and ways of life, with potentially damaging consequences for local and indigenous contexts. Thermal

monotony, in other words, might work to purify indigenous and culturally distinctive ways of living, with climatically as well as culturally damaging implications for the locality itself.

Berndnaut Smilde, *Nimbus Cukurcuma Hamam II*, 2012, c-type print on diabond.

What is crucial to the future is the promise of adaptation and perhaps the placing of faith, as Heschong would put it, not in monotony but 'in the things that provide a little liveliness for us'. Indeed, forgetting the carefully controlled environment (humidity, air speed, air temperature and backlight) needed to achieve it, the Dutch artist Berndnaut Smilde's *Nimbus* series (2010–12) of internal clouds provide incredible wonder and enormous delight as temporary atmospheric events. His clouds only really survive in the images that record them before they disappear forever, but they express the changeability, liveliness and serendipity of air. They inspire a sense of the good fortune to see the wispy radiant shapes, or the bad luck to encounter a rain cloud in an art gallery.

6 Dust to Dust

If death has a smell it must be this.[1]

The dust came first

Dust had grounded Donald Maitland, J. G. Ballard's main character in *The Wind From Nowhere*.[2] Forced to return from London Airport after waiting 48 hours for his Pan Am flight to Montreal, for three long days aircraft were unable to leave the runway. The terminal was 'clogged' with thousands of other passengers stuck in the queues. Unlike Ballard's later paean to the airport, his gestures of freedom, cosmopolitanism and possibility are present only in their loss in his first novel.[3] Life has been grounded by a deadly wind, opportunities closed off, the passenger is merely 'prospectic'. All departures, Maitland finds out later, have been 'indefinitely suspended'.[4]

The year 2010 saw another moment of dust, specifically ash particles which effectively grounded almost all transatlantic air travel to Europe for over a week. The disruption was caused by the eruption of Icelandic volcano Eyjafjallajökull, whose airborne tephra (fine particles of volcanic ash) clogged European airspace, creating the greatest shutdown in global air traffic since 9/11. Previous aircraft guidelines subscribed to a zero-level concentration density for volcanic ash, which was later revised to 4 milligrams per cubic metre of airspace. In Ballard's London the event is almost impossible not to notice as the maelstrom of wind and matter cover everywhere in a layer of dust. Jets of air blow out windows and flood the most sheltered seaside towns. In contrast, the Icelandic aerial event is far more intangible. Lily Ford would

The Eyjafjallajökull ash cloud, 2010.

note the irony since, as the volcano's difficult-to-pronounce name remained unspoken, the ashes were largely unsighted.[5]

Maybe there was a 'silver lining' to the events. As the sky was hushed and shushed, even 'cleaned', the United Nations Environment Programme (UNEP) would note that the event meant the avoidance of about 344×106 kg of CO_2 emissions per day from aircraft fuel, while the volcano emitted about 150×106 kg of CO_2 per day. Britain's Poet Laureate, Carol Ann Duffy, perfectly expressed the juxtaposition of ruined plans, holidays on hold, difficult absences and responsibilities suspended. Duffy asks whether we might find a moment to enjoy our exclusion from the international airways, to hear the birdsong often drowned out by aircraft.[6]

Medium

In *Death at Broadcasting House* (1934), the novel by Val Gielgud and Holt Marvell, former head of production and drama at the BBC, one of the main actors is strangled to death live on air

during the broadcast of a radio play.[7] The murder, as the title suggests, takes place at Broadcasting House, Portland Place, in London, which happened to be the first air-conditioned building in London and furnished with an advanced system by the famous Carrier Corporation of the United States. The building embodies the mediated communication of voice and information on the radio ether. Broadcasting House is seen as the heart of the 'musical life of the British Empire'.

In Gielgud and Marvell's book, the live murder is transported by the airwaves, dangerously penetrating the homes of the population by bringing the insides of Broadcasting House to the listeners' firesides. Murder can go anywhere, yet the contradiction so well explored in *Death* is that the building was utterly insulated from air, atmosphere and sound. An internal encasement, it was a coffin of air. Carrier would use the phrase 'Perfect atmosphere, makes perfect broadcasting possible.'[8]

Carrier's booklet about the building is an image of aura, the building a beacon of light sharply emitting itself out of the darkness. The death, registered in the mediated world of the radio, thus reminds of the double use of the word 'medium'. In the one sense we have the medium of the building's sophisticated sound recording and programme production, and in the other, in ideas of spiritualism. As the building's antennae apparently make connections to other worlds as well as to other places, Broadcasting House is bound up in the air of the dead.

In *Death*, the building takes on an air of the uncanny. The many surfaces, rooms and cubicles now offer the potential for murderous mystery, opened up to the ear of the public. The building's technologies give the appearance of having their own motive force, the ghost in the machine. And outside the glare of the studio lights the shadows are long, corners holding untold secrets. The silence of the muffling decor gives an eerie feel to things.

Broadcasting House, London.

In the far corner, almost under the microphone standard, lay a man's figure unnaturally crumpled . . . Behind the three of them the door shut automatically. 7c was a studio with special

175

acoustic treatment removing all natural echo, and at that moment Rodney Fleming felt acutely the oppressive, almost sinister atmosphere of the room with its single shaded light, its thick carpet and queerly padded walls. The ventilation was perfect, but he felt wanted to draw unusually deep breaths.[9]

Broadcasting House splits opinions on its air. The technological mastery of atmosphere becomes almost oppressive in Gielgud and Holt's novel, while for those looking in at the technological achievement, the building astounds for its prowess over air.

The building was built like a castle. The inner keep was a construction of a single, separate concrete shaft, creating a tower of separated and insulated rooms and studios, cut off from one another to ensure there was no interference of sound or air between recordings. Finished in 1932 and designed by Lt Col. G. Val Myer, the building did not even have any interior light wells, all inner rooms would have to depend on artificial lighting and ventilation. Herman Klein's article in *The Gramophone and the Singer* described the ultimate control over sound and air as 'amazing'; and, while the silence can be actually oppressive, the atmosphere never can be so', fresh air greeting the inhabitants on all levels.[10] The studios were envisaged as enclosures with air as their prisoner. Insulating the studios would do the same to the heat generated by the occupants and the hot lights that illuminated them. Thus Carrier had to produce a ready supply of fresh air and maintain optimum levels of temperature and humidity, all while avoiding the transmission of sound from one studio to another for the sake that their operation needed to be as silent as a mouse.[11]

Carrier installed 32 fans which handled in turn 614 tonnes of air per hour. Sixteen water pumps plus 54 electric motors were used to generate a total horsepower of 504 h.p. 60 independent automatic controls were distributed from the main control room to other parts of the building, linked together by over 120 tonnes of steel ducting. Dampers, arrestors, filters, anti-vibration materials, pumps, fans, sprays and coolers, all these measures and more were used to produce the automatically controlled 'conditioned air'.

In the subsequent Phoenix Film version of Gielgud's book, directed by Reginald Denham in 1934, Gielgud himself plays the producer Julian Caird. At the start of the film we see Caird telling Sydney Parsons (the eventual victim) that he really must get more 'atmosphere into it'.[12] 'Can't you understand', Caird explains, 'that I want the public to think that they can see the murderer's hands throttling the life out of you?' The camera pushes into a lasting shot on Caird's grasping hands before cutting to the next scene.

The 'capsularization' of Broadcasting House means that the murder goes unnoticed for at least ten minutes, although production continues even when the body is found. We hear and see the strangulation. The viewer witnesses the hands creep round Caird's neck, but the sound engineers think his choking is all part of the play, *Murder Immaculate*. A producer or sound engineer gives his colleague a thumbs-up at the realistic performance. We see the crumpled body on the floor of the studio, the murderer's shadow passes and the film cuts to the orchestra who take the signalled queue to play.

What we witness in these moments, continuing as the film began by mixing orchestral music with the beeps of the BBC signal and imagery of the broadcasting aerial, is a sense of synesthesia – a mixture of messages. Broadcasting House expertly insulates air but it also separates and distils, finessing air and sound from the people and machines that produce them to perform an unsettling, uncanny feeling. Different mediums of air, from the airwaves to the air conditioning system, to the sound of the strangulation of the man, seem to come together unnaturally.

Such a Gothic sensibility of breath, sound and death is not uncommon. In fact, the spiritualism Broadcasting House alluded to has had a close association with elements of the aerial uncanny that cinema has tried to represent. *The Others* (2001), an imaginative revival of Henry James's *The Turn of the Screw*, first published in 1898, uses the sound of breathing to cross between the world of the ghosts and the living. Two children, their mother (played by Nicole Kidman) and the servants of the house all suffer together in a half light of candles (on account of the children's skin disorder), and the ghosts of the old house that seem to haunt them. Another world crosses into their own through the conduits of the seance, signalled by the heavy breathing of a blind medium. It is only on seeing the medium that we understand that it is the mother, the children and the servants who are in fact the spirits. It was the mother who killed her children. The fog which had surrounded the house and the countryside with an uncomfortable blanket of distorted shapes and distractions draws back at the film's end to reveal the clarity of their situation. The 'Others' are in fact the new and quite alive owners of the house perturbed by the haunting.

These sorts of expressive qualities of breath and atmosphere are common in the popular imagination. Indeed, the use of breath and sound became a particular tendency in late nineteenth-century spiritualism, which, like the strange effects of Broadcasting House, served to diffuse and disassociate air from sound and body. The Victorian seance sees the female medium 'enveloping' the spectator or participant in a kind of aerial, and very much shared, sonorous space. During the seance, the medium suffused herself into the space of the room, a mobility of air and sound moving in and out of the body, the room becoming 'so to speak, *full*' of a medium like the famous Mrs Guppy.[13] The medium's moaning and heavy breathing would combine with other strange effects. Later representations of possession have also portrayed a similar fascination for atmosphere. For instance in *The Exorcist*, Regan is a girl possessed by the Devil. Her deep and quickening hyperventilating breath merges with the mother's hissing iron. The breath of the priest Karas is visible in the cooled film set, and the windows of the house mist up and clouds emerge as if hot steam or smoke born from the hellish possession.

Suspended air, then, is a familiar tool of storytellers to generate atmospheres of confusion and especially fear. Unlike the medium's occupation of the (usually) domestic space of the seance's setting, villainous male characters tend to melt into the outside air, becoming elemental and fearsome, looming, disappearing, emerging and threatening; they penetrate internal volumes. Picking up on some of the most famous of these, Bram Stoker's eponymous character in *Dracula* (1897) takes the form of air or mist: 'He can come in mist' which he creates. As mist or rays of dust he makes himself 'so small'. It is in this form that the count terrorizes Lucy and later Mina, who lies half asleep and alone in her room behind the French windows. It dawns on Mina that the environment around her is different. The air is 'heavy, dank and cold'. Objects and the light appear harder to make out through the fog which achieves almost material presence as it pours into the room. The mist becomes more like smoke, moving with the energy of boiling water, coming in through the gaps in the joinery of the door. Growing thicker, the smoke concentrates and moves from a flow to accumulating on a spot on the floor. It builds and rises like a pillar of cloud. Two red eyes begin to form in the pillar, before a pale white face bending over her from the darkness is all that she remembers.

The telling of air through the epistolary format of Stoker might compare with the literature of the detective and the amateur sleuth as developed by Wilkie Collins, famous for his experimental style, and Sir Arthur Conan Doyle. Doyle was himself an ardent spiritualist: 6,000 people attended his public seance on 13 July 1930 at the Royal Albert Hall, six days after his death. Doyle had written *The Poison Belt* about a volume of poisonous gas in space through which the earth would pass.[14] Yet in Doyle's rendering of the fog-soaked 'Grimpen Mire' of Baskerville's Devon moor, there is the calculative and rational mind of the detective combating the fog that muddies up the afterlife. Fog signifies the contingencies and uncertainties of even the best-made plans, where Devon could easily be the confusing mists of Crythin Gifford in books such as Susan Hill's *The Woman in Black* that repeatedly use airy atmospheric presence to terrify. The sounds of the horse and trap in the mist; the screams of the drowning pony. The detective figure often moves in atmospheres that creep and curl, disguise and disorientate, emerging from the fog, from air.[15]

Resuscitation

It is October 1795 and Mary looks down from Putney Bridge
in London. She had gone first to Battersea, but there were too
many people around. Mary walks upriver and arrives in Putney
by nightfall. The rain comes down and drenches her figure so that
the clothes cling to her body. Alone, she waits for half an hour
before throwing herself from the bridge.

The writer Mary Wollstonecraft has left a note, hoping that
she would not be 'insulted by being "snatched from death"'.[16]
Forlorn at the breakdown of her relationship with Gilbert Imlay,
the stricken Mary chooses death over life. But Mary does not
sink nor drown straight away. She is forced to wrap her evening
dress around her to lose buoyancy and find suffocation. William
Godwin, her later husband and author of her memoirs, identifies in Mary a 'preternatural action of a desperate spirit'.[17]
Robert Southey, so enamoured with Wollstonecraft, would
accuse Godwin of 'stripping his dead wife naked' in his portrayal
which gives us so much detail of Mary's suicide attempt.[18] And
it becomes just an attempt. Men boating on the river soon race
to meet her and pull her body on board. She was resuscitated by
techniques encouraged by the Royal Humane Society to see
death as but a providential suspension of life, apt to be restored
by breathing air back into the body. In Mary's own words, however, the very act was less than charitable as she was 'inhumanly
brought back to life and misery'.[19]

The Royal Humane Society was an eighteenth-century
society concerned with souls who had drowned or were found
'in which the vital functions are suspended'. It wondered how
to bring them back: why not through that gift of life, breath?
These concerns were not new. In 1767, a Dutch society sent
forth a memoir on practices of resuscitation, a plea for the
saving of life after accidents of all kinds, especially drowning.
The memoir stirred up interest in other countries. Measures
included the inflation of the lungs, drying and warming the body,
rubbing the skin, and sending vapours and smells up the nostrils.
In Britain, these ideas were contemplated and developed further

by the society that had published some of the first kinds of pieces of advice which had saved Mary's life. The society was first known as the 'Society for Affording Immediate Relief to Persons Apparently Dead from Drowning', which formed in 1774.[20] Air as vital spirit seemed to be the problem and the solution, but it was not all that easy to shake off some of the darker tones of snatching a life from death.

Religious stories and myths had dominated folkloric tales of miraculous resuscitation, the most famous being the biblical story of Elisha's death and rebirth: 'He went up, and lay upon the child, and put his mouth upon his mouth . . . and the child opened his eyes.'[21] No blowing or breathing is mentioned in this story, apart from the warmth of his body passed on by the kiss. Other theories propagated included Julius Sperber's *Mysterium Magnum*, published in German in 1660. This supposed that the reanimation of dead people by drowning or suffocating – the 'spark of life' – could be rekindled by a strong

R. Pollard, *A Man Brought in by Boat Apparently Drowned,* 1787, engraving.

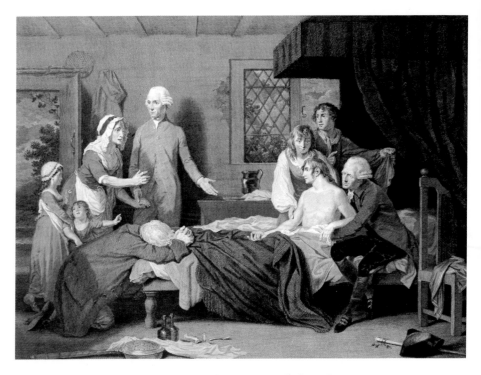

stream of air into the lungs. Yet other theories pervaded newborn or *neonatus* treatments that involved artificial respiration as well as the rubbing of spirits, garlic, onion or mustard to the head, temples and breasts.[22]

R. Pollard, *A Man Recuperating in a Receiving House*, 1787, engraving.

Philosophers and physicians had previously tried to revive animals either under dissection or using procedures such as a tracheotomy, intubations and ventilation. The Roman Galen had led the way in many respects in his 'On the causes of respiration', despite believing that it was air which cooled and ventilated the heart's vital heat. It was the Flemish anatomist Vesalius who had first documented his insertion of a tube into the throat of a mammal which he gently blew air through in 1543. In 1783 one M. de Poiteau advised tracheotomy in artificial respiration, reinflating the lungs through a tube. Debates had waged over whether mouth-to-mouth or the 'kiss of life' was advantageous over the use of bellows. Other dissenting perspectives suggested that mouth-to-mouth might pollute the body – and the Royal

Humane Society would temporarily drop its use in 1812, perhaps seeing breath as if the exhaust of a fire or chimney. And yet, mouth-to-mouth was certainly preferable to other methods of blowing air in. Despite these debates, the society's advice became widespread and it awarded notable performers of resuscitation with medals. Alexander I, tsar of Russia, was awarded a medal in 1806 for helping to save a young man found drowned in the River Neris, while Bram Stoker would win the bronze medal in 1882 after trying to save a man who had jumped into the Thames.

Theories over resuscitation were wide and varied, but all eventually came back to the role of air in the vital motion of the body. For the Yorkshire physician John Fothergill, the lungs could be compared to a pendulum in a clock, ready to be reinflated and kick-started by human action, all in order to 'enable this *Something* to resume the Government of the Fabric, and actuate its Organs afresh'.[23] In this line of thought, the body's spark is equated to that of a machine's original motive force, as indicated in Andreas Vesalius's sixteenth-century, seven-volume anatomy of the human body. The more mechanistic and practical treatments pursued by the society sought to combat the practice's more ghoulish associations. As Benjamin Hawes explained during his speech at the 47th anniversary of the society's founding in 1821, their activities should be understood as a scientific experiment. Their purpose was not 'to raise the dead to life, but to snatch the lifeless from an early grave'.[24] Their emphasis on suspended animation attempted to remove the associations with the unnatural resurrection of a dead life.

The Society built 400 receiving stations in London alone which were constructed according to resuscitative principles and appointed with an 'apparatus' of restoring technologies and techniques as well as ice boats and ladders. Artificial respiration could be conducted by anyone. Restorative potential became the property of the breath of the community, institutions like the Humane Society and those persons willing to administer it, thereby removing the expert oversight of air and life from the domains of science, medicine and even the divine.

Mouth-to-mouth resuscitation the society argued, 'may possibly do great Good, but cannot do harm'.

W. I. Bicknell, *The Receiving Station on the Serpentine, Hyde Park*, 1850, engraving.

Resuscitation could be helped by the right weathers, and some of these were manufactured. Open air was considered the best treatment. The receiving stations were designed to be conducive to resuscitative thermal atmospheres and were armed with a variety of equipment. Central heating with hot water pipes lined the two main treatment rooms of the Serpentine building that would keep a constant equal temperature, without smoke. In case of drowning, the body would be placed in the bath and, if revived, taken to the beds which had copper bottoms filled with hot water to warm the body. A galvanic battery and an artificial respirator would be provided and could be administered if needed.

In spite of the society's efforts, even into the mid-nineteenth century artificial resuscitation was considered strange and ghoulish. Neonatal resuscitation practices appeared odd and macabre; swinging the infant upside down in the Schultze method; squeezing the chest; raising and lowering the arms, rhythmic traction of the tongue, tickling the chest, mouth or throat, 'yelling; shaking' and even 'dilating the rectum using a raven's beak'.[25]

Thomas Hood's poem 'The Bridge of Sighs' (1844) would go on to express a wider trend in Victorian London, and was taken up in more popular representations to portray women's suicides – *fallen* women. Hood's poem described a 'despairing, solitary' figure that reverberates with Mary Wollstonecraft's stricken fall. Within this framing, Mary's leap into the Thames is not necessarily a tragedy because entering the water becomes a purification of 'her sinful habits'. In these representations, water cleanses. It signifies rebirth and, thus, treatment by air becomes unnecessary, should it spoil the redemptive and sexualized portrayal of the woman's body.

Whilst the society's techniques and ideas essentially remade the corpse into a half-life promising a return to health, in much of the imagery and stories that are associated with 'The Bridge of Sighs', as pictured in Watts's famous painting *Found Drowned* (c. 1848–50), none account for attempts of resuscitation. This

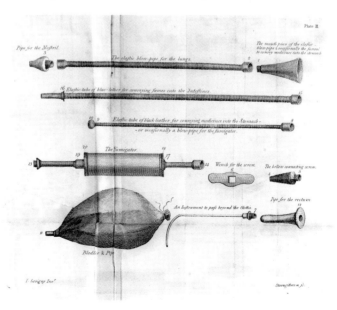

Savigny, *Instruments for the Recovery of the Apparently Dead*, 1788, engraving.

is surprising, given the popularity of the Humane Society's pamphlets and advice. Yet if death is believed redemptive and is told through the necrophilic excitement we have seen, the holding of the corpse in beatific composure cannot be spoiled, even by resuscitative air. The face is lovely, written with a placid smile. The skin is luxuriant and holds a melancholy pallor. Purified by the water, any recovery due to the dirty breath of a passer-by would simply be immoral.

Mary Wollstonecraft would try to commit suicide on two further occasions, although she never again attempted to drown herself. She died following the difficult birth of her daughter, Mary Shelley, in 1797. Clearly, resuscitation and the Promethean myth are obvious themes in Mary Shelley's most famous work *Frankenstein* (1818), whose creation is brought to life in the book. Frankenstein himself is also revived by warming. In parallel, Mary's life seems to have been greatly disturbed by suicides and resuscitation. Her husband was Percy Bysshe Shelley, whose first wife, Harriet, had drowned herself in the Serpentine lake in 1816. Estranged from her husband, and heavily pregnant with another man's baby, it is believed she reached the lake via the Fox and Bull Inn. The wooden gate at the back opened onto Hyde Park and a path that led to the lake. Ironically, this was

George Frederic Watts, *Found Drowned*, 1848–50, oil on canvas.

the same entrance through which bodies of persons drowned in the Serpentine were conveyed to the inn, which operated as the secondary receiving station of the Royal Humane Society on the south side of Hyde Park, where Harriet's body was immediately taken.[26]

It was some time until consensus was eventually achieved over mouth-to-mouth. The Austrian physician Peter Safar and the respiratory researcher James Elam, following their research on resuscitation techniques, saw their methods taken up by the National Academy of Scientists in 1958 and the publication of several pamphlets on the technique led to its widespread adoption. Safar and Elam would also go on to work with Norwegian toy manufacturer Asmund Laerdal to create Resusci Anne, or CPR Annie, to simulate the human respiratory system. The doll, or some variant of it, continues to be used in first aid instruction and training today.

Air/war

War, as we have seen, is not just fought from the air, but it is in the air too. Britain's experience of the Second World War would see writers making sense of the deterioration of life on the home front. Their premise: that life had regressed, wasting away in putrefaction. In Max Nordau's *Degeneration*, the atmosphere is charged with decay, inhaled.[27] War brought to Britain a kind of literature which described the fever of things gone bad, places going off. The munitions factories drip with Gothic descriptions of strange light and the working conditions without windows or sealed without ventilation. This 'hell' of industry is configured in several ways. We see women's labour brought into a familiar relation with the exotic as the factory is compared to an oriental market. Elsewhere, war artist Graham Sutherland represents the cave-like surroundings of the foundry in *Tapping a Blast Furnace* (1941–2), which seems more like the lair of a dragon whose throat can be seen exhaling fire and smoke. This is hell through hot air and fire, heat and glare. Under these conditions, society has been brought back to something primitive, strange and even ghoulish. Away from the crackle of Sutherland's foundries and mines there is gloom. Light becomes misty, green, almost white. Compared to a tomb, the air of the war's spaces seems to bring the workers to an even closer relation to the dead.

How to tolerate these airs of war rendered through more Gothic than romantic sensibilities? Jumping ahead 30 years, for Ninh's Vietnamese solider in South Vietnam, Kien, from the novel *The Sorrow of War* (1994), death meant the body liquidized and evaporated. All the souls of the dead penetrate Kien whole, his comrades, strangers, all living inside and aside him and his thoughts: 'with their final breath their souls were released . . . becoming a dark shadow overhanging his own soul'.[28] Like the 'Agent Orange' dioxin compounds dropped as a fine and powdery mist on the jungle to defoliate its canopy, the air of war seems to persist in the long-lasting ghosts of conflict.

For Kien, those who died continued to live in him as if oxygen suffused into his blood. Kien would retrieve the memories through the images and sensations that haunted him. The valve to release those thoughts and experiences was writing. Kien remembers the helicopter raids attacking overhead, the 'dreaded whump-whump-whump-whump of their rotor blades'. But the 'whump-whump-whump' continues, detached from the attack, the images soon dissolve and in their place is the ceiling fan of his apartment, going 'Whump-whump-whump'. In these moments his memories and projections seem to take on an air of themselves, possessing the air of the room that somehow now feels 'strange, vibrating with images of the past'. His walls shake noisily as jets go on their bombing runs.[29]

The shiny canisters of napalm falling from the American planes turn everything into a soup of turbulence and chaos as Kien and his girlfriend Phuong are caught up in a raid. Even a camp scene by the lake is unmade as the wind whips up spray from the water-body; blankets, towels, pegs are all caught up in the attack. The air seems to crack like broken glass, the earth 'heaving under them, then falling again'. In another raid, the pressure wave hits like a punch in the face. Kien grabs Phuong's hand and their fingers entangle. The surreal landscape of the

Asmund Laerdal demonstrates Resusci Anne.

war's ending Kien describes like a deflation, the violence that holds everything up is lost, but the ghosts remain and stay with Kien. The corpse of a girl from Saigon Airport which is treated so horrifically by another soldier dissolves into his apartment, which goes up like smoke, replaced by an apparition of the naked girl again, 'her hair messy, her dark eyes swarming with ants, and on her lips a terrible twisted smile'.[30] Phuong sings a song to a group of soldiers. Echoing Bob Dylan, perhaps it could be a scene from Francis Ford Coppola's *Apocalypse Now* (1979). The air is sung with a melancholic sense of certainty that something is about to alter: 'The winds, they are a changin'.

In Ballard's *Empire of the Sun* (1984), Jim is wandering among the strange and deserted aerodrome, abandoned by the Chinese for the invading Japanese Army. This was a place of magic, recovering and recalls a nostalgic memory of the fantasies of flight we started with, 'where the air ran with dreams and excitements'. Gone are the gloom and solemnity of the Blitz,

Atmospheres of the Vietnam War, near Cantho, 1967.

or the madness in Vietnam, in this moment. Jim wades into the waist-high grass surrounding the aerodrome. It is like water with a 'warm surface, and a cooler sub-layer touched by mysterious currents'.[31] The grass dances in the wind, mimicking the glider he would soon release 'like the slipstreams of invisible aircraft'. Jim finds a decaying Japanese fighter plane. Putting his balsa model on the aircraft, he lowers himself into the seat and sits among the dead pilot now lying on the floor of the cockpit. The air here buzzes with the past, of atmospheres potent with a nostalgia which 'hovered over the cockpit'. Jim climbs on the engine cowling. He picks up his glider and launches it into the air, and as it catches the wind 'the model banked steeply and soared'.

Human smoke

Frédéric Beigbeder's novel *Windows on the World* (2003) gives a fictional account of the restaurant at the World Trade Center during its last moments of existence. A character explains how the smoke moved, seeping from the floor. It comes from everywhere, 'the ventilation system becomes a fumigation system'.[32]

The events of 9/11 marked an astonishingly apt collision. Martin Amis notes how the two technological forms that first brought life to the air – the aeroplane and the skyscraper – in this moment kill it.[33] On 11 September 2001 they clashed utterly and obviously so violently that what was left was not simply the nothingness of the gap left in the sky – an absence – but at least for a time, a huge column of smoke and dust. The towers, aircraft, inhabitants and thousands of rescue workers were violently transformed into an enormous mountain of rubble streaming up and down to form huge pillars of smoke, ash, dust and collapsing structures that were visible from space. Many of the victims were never accounted for because their bodies were no longer whole. From hands to feet, bodies were pulverized or, for Amis, 'pestled'. Individuals were made indistinguishable.[34] The result had been anticipated in Rachel Whiteread's *Demolished* (1996), as the dust looked much like an arm pushing out from the earth to claw at the sky, so suggestive of the kinds of twentieth- and twenty-first-century atmospheric threats to follow.

Temporarily, at least, people and buildings became air. Phased into infinitesimal bits of dust, 9/11 brought the enormous structures and its inhabitants into the air, the event performed the physical sublimation of phase from solid into gaseous state. For Don DeLillo, there was ash and paper everywhere, paper whipping through the air, no sign of light or sky. This kind of minimalism is echoed in Hartmut Bitomsky's strange movie about dust that looks at the terrible composition of air following the World Trade Center's collapse. From 'mineral wool . . . cellulose . . . polyaromats . . . metal particles like copper . . . mercury, chrome, aluminum . . . cement, lime . . . arsenic, cadmium . . . paraffin, airplane fuel'.[35] The dust was touched, people breathed it in, they swallowed it, tried to remove it from their clothes and hair, carpets, sofas and teddy bears. Over 18,000 people have suffered from respiratory problems in the wake of the events leading to the recent Zadroga Act (2010), which signed into law $4.3 billion of aid for 9/11 victims.

Almost as soon as the dust was beginning to settle in the few days following the events of that September, numerous studies began to investigate the composition of the air inhaled by the public and rescue workers. Several of these projects were delayed because of the problem of the human in the air. As journalists asked just what the World Trade Center's dust cloud was made of, Paul J. Lioy – one of the chief researchers involved in the study – had to deal with the question of whether DNA could be identifiable from their samples.[36] What the question came down to, as well as the sensitivity of the matter of air, was whether the scientists would require approval for the use of human samples in their tests. As it happened they did not. Despite the chance of discovering identifiable DNA from the dust samples residing somewhere near the quadrillionth percentile, law requires that medical research only seek permission if the sample of human tissue is actually alive. As with Bitomsky, this is a subtraction of an emotion. But maybe this is another way of coping with an air whose violence becomes too much, as the enormity of the

billowing matter pushes at the limits of expression. This is not so uncommon when air becomes what has been called a kind of 'human smoke'.

Many years before, Paul Goyard was a celebrated French stage designer deported to the Buchenwald concentration camp on 14 May 1944. Goyard describes his experience of one morning. He sees an automated machine of death, as people and bodies he does not know become 'human smoke' on an industrial scale in the Nazi Final Solution.[37] In *Naissance d'un jour*, Goyard's poem moves oddly out of the sensuous encounter of landscape, wind, cold and sky to a more spectacular ceremonial stage of a blinding dawn. As Goyard beholds the human smoke spilling out of the death camp's chimneys he explains, 'This is how in this city of hell men ascend to heaven', a sentiment echoed by others, such as Paul Celan in his 'Death Fugue' (1948).[38]

Writing soon after the conflict, Edward Abbey found it difficult not to see Europe in these sorts of terms, as a giant crematorium on a much larger scale than the Nazi camps, urbanizing the Nazi killing machine to city-as-furnaces fuelled by Allied incendiary bombs.[39] Ironically, the human smoke of the Holocaust fulfilled an older anti-Semitic figure of the *Luftmenschen*, or airman – a sometimes derogatory gesture to the rootless and apparent superfluousness of the Jewish diaspora.[40]

Such suffering provokes writer Edward Abbey's anger. He cannot but help reveal his disgust at the people living 'without room to breathe' together and trapped. We might even compare this with how Germany's streets were 'converted into jets', how the 'air was burning', the city and its atmosphere ignited by a perfect storm of incendiary bombs and weather conditions which, on the night of 28 July 1943, turned Hamburg into a hurricane of gas, sparks and ferociously hot air.[41] This was not the moment for shelter. Almost the reverse of the Twin Towers' implosive collapse, grinding buildings, bodies and cremation, Hamburg's unusual weather conditions turned the fire into a hurricane. Superheating the air above the city, a chain reaction began which started sucking all the oxygen and cooler air from within the city and its surrounding area in order to feed itself. Shooting skywards to almost 6,095 m (20,000 ft) as it heated, the fire brought wind speeds in the city up to over 193 km/h (120 mph). Channelled by the city's streets, temperatures reached 1,400°C (2,552°F), melting buildings and people, suffocating others trapped in cellars and shelters. Abbey's reaction is understandable. He sees an atmosphere of such 'ugliness and hatred' but so 'all-pervasively seeping' that it penetrated his writing, 'it has gotten into my ink . . . My God!'[42]

Sky burial

Perhaps air is an end. In Phillip Pullman's *His Dark Materials* trilogy, a gas lamp fantasy with Victorian pneumatics and airships galore, it is air and dust that people eventually become. The character Lyra explains that 'You'll drift apart, it's true, but you'll be out in the open, part of everything alive again.'[43] Perhaps this is compatible with the Tibetan sky burial practice of *jhator*, where a corpse is dissected and divided in the open, to be ultimately given back to the skies and the birds and the air.

These endings help us to remember the poignancy of Luce Irigaray's essential claim, a claim of the communal character of air; borne once into it, air is what we ultimately become.[44] For if we are at all to live together now, on this Earth and in the shared air, we should remember, as DeLillo explained, that we are all breathing in the loss and the suffering and the bodies lost in the event that have turned into the air. Air *is* a sharing, the experience of those watching the air pump and the canary's croaks of Joseph Wright's depiction. Even the dead are to be found, quite simply, everywhere, 'in the soft breeze off the river, on rooftops and windows, in our hair and on our clothes'.[45]

Around and essentially of us and in us.

y burial ground
Tibet.

TIMELINE

3.5 billion years ago   Oxygen levels began to increase in the planet's atmosphere as organic life forms converted carbon dioxide into oxygen.

300 million years ago During the Carboniferous period, an oxygen spike occurred which saw enormous carbon deposits buried in swamps and insect giganticism.

Sixth century BC   In Ionia, Ancient Greece, philosophers debate the existence of air as an element.

1347   Gentile da Foligno presents his *Consilium contra pestilentiam*, or *Consilium*, a work on plague, its causes – often by bad airs and miasmas – and remedies.

1643   Evangelista Torricelli invents the barometer and builds the first of its kind in 1644.

1652   Robert Burton's extraordinary *Anatomy of Melancholy* is posthumously published, outlining a humoural examination of the temperament.

1654   Otto von Guericke demonstrates his Magdeburg hemisphere experiment at Regensburg, proving the existence of atmospheric pressure, or the weight of air.

1661   John Evelyn publishes a warning to London's Whitehall residents on the insalubrity of the air tainted by the river Thames.

1775   Marsilio Landriani publishes his *Physical Investigations on the Salubrity of Air*, a landmark work in eudiometry that outlines his design for the eudiometer.

1784   Vincenzo Lunardi makes his first balloon flight from the Honourable Artillery Company Ground in London.

1788   Jacques Tenon publishes his memoirs on air, miasmas and the management of hospital treatment.

1774   Joseph Priestley's experiments on burning mercury oxide lead him to the discovery of 'dephlostigated air', oxygen.

1789   French aristocrat-scientist Antoine Lavoisier publishes *Traité élémentaire de chimie*, splitting air into constitutive gases, and transforms modern chemistry.

1792   Priestley's house is stormed at Fairhill following the Birmingham Riots. His house is razed to the ground, the laboratories ruined.

1794   Georgiana Cavendish, Duchess of Devonshire, sponsors Blanchard's balloon flight from Grosvenor Square in London. A military observation balloon is used successfully at Fleurus by the French Revolutionary Army.

1832   Europe newspapers begin reporting of a Madras Brahmin who is promised to be able to levitate.

1844   J.M.W. Turner finishes his *Rain, Steam and Speed*, depicting a remarkable confluence of air, colour and industry in the railway's annihilation of space by time. Engels publishes his treatise on the working conditions of the

English working class, focusing on their unhealthy airs.

1852   Henry Mayhew makes his famous balloon ascent over London.

1855   The Swiss physical Arnold Rickli coins the term 'atmospheric bath' to describe his air treatment for sufferers of tuberculosis. Elizabeth Gaskell publishes *North and South*, a story of a woman's social and geographical mobility to a polluted northern town.

1871   Famous for his time-motion chrono-photography, Étienne-Jules Marey begins publishing his experimental studies on birds following his earlier work on smoke. Frank H. Wenham designs the first wind tunnel.

1881   Birdsill Holley patents the world's first steam radiator, starting a steam heat craze as several American cities are built with vast underground steam pipes.

1889   The Eiffel Tower is built for the Paris World's Fair. Its architect and inventor Gustave Eiffel installs various meteorological equipment in the tower to measure air and wind resistance.

1904   The Louisiana Purchase Exposition features on its main thoroughfare – *the Pike* – John Zahorsky's baby incubator exhibit.

1907   The Queen Alexandra Sanatorium is completed in Davos, Switzerland. A modern version of the terraced sanatorium chalet design encourages air and sunlight immersion.

1911   John Scott Haldane performs his ground-breaking altitude experiments on Pikes Peak, Colorado.

1915   At Ypres the German army releases the first poison gas cloud made up of chlorine against

French forces. Haldane soon follows to examine
the effects on the French troops. *Civilization and
Climate* is published by Yale Geography Professor
Ellsworth Huntingdon. The Carrier Engineering
Corporation is formed, one of the world's first
producers of air conditioners.

1920   The National Advisory Committee for
Aeronautics (NACA) builds the atmospheric wind
tunnel at Langley Field, Virginia – then the
largest windtunnel in the world.

1927   Charles Lindbergh crosses the Atlantic and lands
at Le Bourget near Paris before returning
triumphantly to a tickertape parade in New York.

1929   The first baby girl is born in the air, above Miami,
Florida. She is named Airlene.

1936   Salvador Dalí almost suffocates himself to death
within the sealed atmosphere of a diving suit
during a Surrealist exhibition. He was trying to
dive into the unconscious.

1938   America begins its Civilian Pilot Training
Programme. Tullio Crali paints his famous
Dogfight Futurist artwork.

1950   A decade later, 1950 becomes significant for the
denotation B.P. (before present). Testing atomic
weapons in the Pacific means that radiocarbon
dating after 1950 is unreliable.

1960   Willard F. Libby wins the Nobel Prize in
Chemistry for inventing carbon dating. Oil is
discovered in Dubai, which would later permit
one of the world's most excessively air
conditioned spaces.

1961   Yves Klein presents his Architecture de l'air or
Air Architecture.

1970   The United States Census is nicknamed the 'air
conditioned census' by the *New York Times*

because of the dramatic effect of the air conditioner on migration patterns to America's Southern states.

1984   The Bhopal disaster sees a leak at the Union Carbide India chemical plant, releasing a toxic gas cloud of methyl isocynate which kills a number estimated between 3,000 and 10,000 of the plant's local residents, making it the worst industrial accident in history.

1988   Several wings are finished at the New York Metropolitan Museum of Art, including the wing holding the Dendur temple. The buildings are the most climatically sophisticated controlled environments in the world.

1991   Bret Easton Ellis's *American Psycho* is published, one of a number of books dissatisfied with the atmosphere of Manhattan's elites fueled by the excesses of finance capital. Biosphere 2 in Arizona, begins its first scientific mission with eight volunteers.

2001   The Eden project opens in Cornwall. The attacks on the World Trade Center create a vast column of ash and dust, while the United States closes its airspace.

2002   Elizabeth Diller and Roberto Scofido open their Blur building on Lake Neuchâtel, Switzerland.

2010   The Eyjafjallajökull volcano in Iceland erupts, creating an ash cloud that closes much of transatlantic and European airspace.

REFERENCES

Introduction

1 Vladimir Jankovic, *Reading the Skies: A Cultural History of English Weather, 1650–1820* (Chicago, 2001), pp. 33–49.
2 James Lovelock and Lynn Margulis, 'Atmospheric Homeostasis By and For the Biosphere: The Gaia Hypothesis', *Tellus*, XXVI/1–2 (1974), pp. 2–10 (p. 2). See also Lovelock, *Gaia: A New Look at Life* (Oxford, 1979).
3 Dian R. Hitchcock and James Lovelock, 'Life Detection by Atmospheric Analysis', *Icarus*, VII/1–3 (1967), pp. 149–59.
4 J.B.S. Haldane, 'On Being the Right Size' (1928), http://irl.cs.ucla.edu.
5 O. von Guericke, in T. Conlon, *Thinking about Nothing: Otto von Guericke and the Magdeburg Experiments on a Vacuum* (London, 2011), p. 227.
6 Robert E. Schofield, *A Scientific Autobiography of Joseph Priestley* (Cambridge, MA, 1966), p. 194.
7 Ibid., p. 184.
8 Steven Johnson, *The Invention of Air: An Experiment, a Journey, a New Country, and the Amazing Force of Scientific Discovery* (London, 2009).
9 Jenny Uglow, *The Lunar Men: The Friends Who Made the Future, 1730–1810* (New York, 2002).
10 The coffee house was becoming the place par excellence for the production of public life and the dissemination of scientific ideas, knowledge and excitement. For Jürgen Habermas, the renowned historical sociologist, these places were new sites of civility. The coffee house atmosphere suspended rank, status and class and the 'aura of extraordinariness' of the court or the Church, allowing Priestley to share and develop his revolutionary scientific ideas with his friends and colleagues.

11 Quoted in Richard R. Chase, 'Jules Michelet and the Nineteenth-century Concept of Insanity: A Romantic's Reinterpretation', *French Historical Studies*, XVII/3 (1992), p. 743.

12 Jules Michelet, *Historical View of the French Revolution: from its Earliest Indications to the Flight of the King in 1791* (London, 1860), p. 53.

13 Charles Dickens, *A Tale of Two Cities* (London, 1859).

14 Ibid., p. 156.

15 Quoted in F. W. Gibbs, *Joseph Priestley: Adventurer in Science and Champion of Truth* (London, 1965), p. 195.

16 Joseph Priestley, *Letters to the Right Honourable Edmund Burke, occasioned by his Reflections on the Revolution in France* (London, 1791); Maurice Crosland, 'The Image of Science as a Threat: Burke versus Priestley and the 'Philosophic Revolution', *British Journal for the History of Science*, XX/3 (1987), pp. 277–307.

17 Henry Mayhew and John Binney, 'Extract from *The Criminal Prisons of London*' (1862) (originally printed in *Illustrated London News*, 18 September 1852).

18 Karl Marx, 'Speech at the Anniversary of the People's Paper', *The People's Paper* (1856), p. 500. I am indebted to Ben Anderson's paper, 'Affective Atmospheres', *Emotion, Space and Society*, II/2 (2009), pp. 77–81, for pointing me to this quote.

19 Karl Marx, *The Poverty of Philosophy* (Paris, 1847).

20 Walter Benjamin, *The Arcades Project* (Cambridge, MA, 1999), p. 125.

21 Michael Adas, *Machines as the Measure of Men* (Ithaca, NY, 1990), p. 223.

22 Enda Duffy, *The Speed Handbook: Velocity, Pleasure, Modernism* (Raleigh and Durham, NC, 2009), p. 11.

23 Marshall Berman, *All that is Solid Melts into Air: The Experience of Modernity* (New York, 1983), p. 237.

24 William Howard Russell, *The Indian Mutiny: My Diary in India* (London, 1858), p. 73.

25 Elizabeth DeLoughrey, 'Radiation Ecologies and the Wars of Light', *Modern Fiction Studies*, LV/3 (Fall 2009), pp. 468–98 (p. 475).

26 Willard F. Libby, 'Radiocarbon Dating', www.nobelprize.org.

27 Ibid.

28 Steven Connor, 'Exhaust' (2006), www.stevenconnor.com.

1 Airborne

1 Steven Connor, *The Matter of Air: Science and the Art of the Ethereal* (London, 2010), p. 9.

2 Various references to this birth attribute the baby's name to 'Aerogene'.

3 Luce Irigaray, *The Forgetting of Air in Martin Heidegger* (Austin, TX, 1999).
4 Scott Palmer, *Dictatorship of the Air* (Cambridge, 2006).
5 Ibid., p. 243.
6 Ibid., p. 154.
7 Joseph Corn, *The Winged Gospel* (Washington, DC, 1993).
8 Ann Douglas, *Terrible Honesty: Mongrel Manhattan in the 1920s* (New York, 1996), p. 434.
9 Ibid.
10 N. L. Engelhardt, 'Air-conditioning Education', *American Association of School Administrators* (Washington, DC, 1944), p. 43.
11 Étienne-Jules Marey, 'Lectures on the Phenomena of Flight in the Animal Kingdom', *Annual Report of the Smithsonian* (1871).
12 Étienne-Jules Marey, 'The Movements of the Wing of Insects', *Annual Reports of the Aeronautical Society* (1872), pp. 25–74.
13 Étienne-Jules Marey, 'The Experimental Study on the Motion of Fluids', *Scientific American* (1902), p. 75.
14 Liz Millward, *Women in British Imperial Airspace, 1922–1937* (Montreal and London, 2007).
15 See the documentary *The Legend of Pancho Barnes and the Happy Bottom Riding Club* (2009), directed by Amanda Pope. The producer and writer is Nick T. Spark and the associate producer is the geographer-pilot Dydia DeLyser.
16 Peter Fritzsche, *A Nation of Flyers* (New York, 1991), p. 122.
17 Antoine de Saint-Exupéry, *Southern Mail; Night Flight*, trans. Curtis Cate (London, 1971), p. 8.
18 Jeffrey T. Schnapp, 'Propeller Talk', *Modernism/Modernity*, I/3 (1994), pp. 153–78 (p. 154).
19 See David Matless, *Landscape and Englishness* (London, 1999).
20 Sefton Brancker, 'Untitled', *RAF Cadet College Gazette* (1920), p. 48.
21 T. E. Lawrence, *The Mint* (London, 1955), p. 200.
22 Ibid., p. 178.
23 Ibid., p. 177.
24 Filippo Tommaso Marinetti, 'The Futurist Manifesto', *Le Figaro* (20 February 1909).
25 Thomas Pynchon, *Against the Day* (New York, 2006), p. 1203.
26 Derek P. McCormack, 'Aerostatic Spacing: On Things Becoming Lighter than Air', *Transactions of the Institute of British Geographers*, XXXIV/1 (2009), pp. 25–41, (p. 28).
27 Dorthe Simonsen, 'The Aviation Neck: Techno-choreographies of Early Flight', *Up in the Air* (2011).
28 Caren Kaplan, 'The Balloon Prospect', in Peter Adey, Alison Williams and Mark Whitehead, *From Above* (forthcoming).

29 Adnan Morshed, 'The Aesthetics of Ascension in Norman Bel
    Geddes's Futurama', *Journal of the Society of Architectural Historians*,
    LXIII/1 (March 2004), pp. 74–99 (p. 93).
30 Jill Jones, *Eiffel's Tower* (New York, 2009).
31 Ibid., p. 153.
32 Georges Eiffel, 'The Eiffel Tower', *Annual Report of the Board
    of Regents of the Smithsonian Institution* (1889), p. 733; see also
    William A. Eddy, 'The Eiffel Tower', *Annual Report of the Board
    of Regents of the Smithsonian Institution* (1889), reprinted from the
    Atlantic Monthly, no. 224, Pt 1, p. 736.
33 'A Long-enduring Nuisance', *New York Times* (22 June 1888),
    p. 9.
34 William James, 'On a Certain Blindness in Human Beings',
    in *Talks to Teachers on Psychology* (Rockville, MD, 2008), p. 126.
35 'Skyscrapers', in Ann Douglas, *Terrible Honesty: Mongrel Manhattan
    in the 1920s* (New York, 1995), pp. 203–4.

2 An Excess of Air

1   Robert Burton, *The Anatomy of Melancholy* (New York, 1870,
    new edition).
2   Marco Beretta, 'Pneumatics vs. "Aerial Medicine": Salubrity and
    Respirability of Air at the End of the Eighteenth Century', *Nuova
    Voltiana: Studies on Volta and His Times*, ed. Fabio Bevilacqua and
    Lucio Fregonese (Pavia and Milan, 2000), pp. 49–71 (p. 59).
3   Simon Schaffer, 'Measuring Virtue: Eudiometry, Enlightenment,
    and Pneumatic Medicine', in *The Medical Enlightenment of the
    Eighteenth Century*, ed. Andrew Cunningham and Roger French
    (Cambridge, 1990), p. 287.
4   Emily Cockayne, *Hubbub: Filth, Noise and Stench in England*
    (Ann Arbor, MI, 2007).
5   David S. Barnes, *The Great Stink of Paris and the Nineteenth-century
    Struggle against Filth and Germs* (Baltimore, MD, 2006), p. 12.
6   Ibid., p. 3.
7   Metropolitan Sewage Committee Proceedings. Parliamentary
    Papers, 1846. p. 10: 651, www.parlipapaers.chadwyck.co.uk.
8   Barnes, *The Great Stink*, p. 97.
9   Patrick Süskind, *Perfume: The Story of a Murderer* (London, 1985).
10 Ibid., p. 3.
11 Michel Foucault, *History of Madness*, trans. Jean Khalfa and
    Jonathan Murphy (New York, 1972), p. 356.
12 Süskind, *Perfume*, p. 17.
13 Elizabeth Gaskell, *North and South* (London, 1855 [repr. 2003]),
    p. 102.

14 Frederick Engels, *The Condition of the Working Class in England in 1844* (London, 1892).

15 P. Gaskell, *The Manufacturing Population of England: Its Moral, Social, And Physical Conditions, and the Changes which have Arisen from the Use of Steam Machinery* (London, 1833).

16 Luke Howard, *The Climate of London* (London, 1833).

17 Timothy Choy, 'Air's Substantiations', Berkeley Environmental Politics Colloquium, 2011, p. 30; see http://globetrotter.berkeley.

18 Naipaul quoted in Mary Douglas, *Purity and Danger: An Analysis of the Concepts Pollution and Taboo* (London, 1966), p. 149.

19 A. B. de Guerville, *New Egypt* (Berlin, 1905); I am indebted to Derek Gregory's writings on de Guerville and this topic. See Derek Gregory, 'Scripting Egypt', in *Writes of Passage: Reading Travel Writing*, ed. Derek Gregory and James Duncan (New York, 1999).

20 De Guerville, *New Egypt*, p. 79; Gregory, 'Scripting', p. 143.

21 Charles Baudelaire, *The Flowers of Evil*, trans. James McCowan (Oxford, 2008), p. 49.

22 Charles Baudelaire, *Paris Spleen*, trans. Martin Sorrell (New York, 2008 [1869]).

23 Constance Classen, *The Colour of Angels: Cosmology, Gender and the Aesthetic Imagination* (New York, 1998), p. 80.

24 Eustace Reynolds-Ball, *The City of the Caliphs: A Popular Study of Cairo and its Environs and the Nile and its Antiquities* (London and Paris, 1897), p. 192.

25 Ibid., p. 90.

26 Constance Gordon-Cumming, *Via Cornwall to Egypt* (London, 1885), p. 293.

27 Reynolds-Ball, *The City*, p. 196.

28 Ibid., p. i.

29 Rafatul Hussaini quoted by Kim Fortun, *Advocacy After Bhopal* (Chicago, 2001), p. 166.

30 Don DeLillo, *White Noise* (New York, 1985 [repr. 1999]), p. 127.

31 Ibid., p. 119.

32 Carl von Clausewitz, *On War* (London, 1873).

33 DeLillo, *White Noise*, p. 139.

34 Ibid., pp. 140–41.

35 Fortun, *Advocacy*, p. 1.

36 Ibid., p. 102.

37 David Gissen, 'The Architectural Production of Nature, Dendur/New York', *Grey Room*, xxxiv (Winter 2009), pp. 58–79.

3 Restoration

1 Gaston Bachelard, *Air and Dreams; An Essay on the Imagination of Movement* (Dallas, TX, 1988).
2 Johanna Spyri, *Heidi* (Philadelphia and London, 1919), p. 270.
3 Friedrich Nietzsche, *Ecce Homo* (Oxford, 2007), p. 22.
4 Ibid., p. 21.
5 Baudelaire, *The Flowers of Evil*, trans. James McCowan (Oxford, 2008), p. 17.
6 Ibid., p. 17.
7 Edward Frankland, 'A Great Winter Sanitarium for the American Continent', *Popular Science Monthly* (1885).
8 Paul Overy, *Light, Air and Openness: Modern Architecture Between the Wars* (London, 2008).
9 Adrien Guignard, 'A "Sanatorial Method" for the Good Alpine and Desert Air', *Revue de Géographie Alpine*, XCIII/1 (2005), pp. 70–79 (p. 71).
10 Rousseau, quoted ibid., p. 72.
11 Norbert Wolf, *Kirchner* (Cologne, 2003) p. 9.
12 Emily Abel, *Tuberculosis and the Politics of Exclusion: A History of Public Health and Migration to Los Angeles* (New Brunswick, NJ, 2007), pp. 6–7.
13 Jane Austen, *Persuasion* (London, 1817), p. 104.
14 Wendy Parkins, *Mobility and Modernity in Women's Novels, 1850s–1930s: Women Moving Dangerously* (Basingstoke, 2009).
15 Alain Corbin, *The Lure of the Sea* (Los Angeles, 1994), p. 268.
16 Ibid., p. 267.
17 Elizabeth Gaskell, *North and South*, p. 76.
18 Classen, *The Color of Angels: Cosmology, Gender and the Aesthetic Imagination* (New York, 1998), p. 66.
19 Gaskell, *North and South*, p. 170.
20 Ibid., p. 177.
21 Michel Foucault, *The Birth of the Clinic*, trans. Alan Sheriden (London, 1973 [2003]).
22 Michel Foucault, 'The Incorporation of the Hospital into Modern Technology', in *Space, Knowledge and Power: Foucault and Geography*, ed. Stuart Elden and Jeremy Crampton (Aldershot, 2007).
23 Guignard, 'A Sanatorial Method'.
24 Tenon in Foucault, 'Incorporation', p. 149.
25 John Burton-Fanning, 'Open-air Treatment of Phthisis in England', *The Lancet* (1898), p. 855.
26 Ibid., p. 854.
27 Ibid., p. 631.

28 Cited in Margaret Campbell, 'What Tuberculosis Did for Modernism: The Influence of a Curative Environment on Modernist Design and Architecture', *Medical History*, XLIX/4 (1 October 2005), pp. 463–88.

29 Ibid., p. 633.

30 Jeffrey Baker, *The Machine in the Nursery: Incubator Technology and the Origins of Newborn Intensive Care* (Baltimore, MD, 1996), p. 144.

31 'Sanitary Wire Cradles for Babies' Sanitarium', *Popular Mechanics* (1917), p. 365.

32 Theodore B. Sachs, *The Municipal Control of Tuberculosis in Chicago: Its History and Provisions* (Chicago, 1915), p. 32.

33 Campbell, 'What Tuberculosis Did for Medicine', p. 483.

34 Susan Sontag, *Illness as Metaphor* (London, 1991), p. 18.

35 David Boyd Haycock, *A Crisis of Brilliance: Five Young Artists and the Great War* (London, 2009).

36 Ibid., p. 288. Gertler, like Kirchner, was also doing all he could to escape enlistment.

37 Ibid., p. 169.

38 Letter and envelope from D. H. Lawrence, Ad Astra, Vence, [Alpes-Maritimes, France] to Mrs Dorothy Morland, Hôtel du Louvre, Menton, [France] DD/791/3A-B, 1930.

39 Letter from D. H. Lawrence, Ad Astra, Vence (Alpes-Maritimes, France) to Dr Andrew Morland (England) DD/791/2, 9 February 1930.

40 Andrew Morland, 'The Mind in Turbercle', *The Lancet* (1932), p. 178.

4 Insulation

1 Tom Wolfe, *Bonfire of the Vanities* (New York, 1991).

2 Martin Goodman, *Suffer and Survive: The Extreme Life of J. S. Haldane* (London, 2007).

3 Paul Bert was Bernard's student and was heavily influential in the understanding of altitude physiology. He made incredibly important observations that have come to directly influence our understanding of the body's interaction at altitude and in flight. Bert's *Barometric Pressure* (Columbus, OH, 1943), was translated for the U.S. Air Force in 1943.

4 Peter Sloterdijk, *Terror From the Air*, trans. Amy Patton and Steve Corcoran (Cambridge, MA, 2008), p. 25.

5 Steven Connor, *The Matter of Air: Science and the Art of the Ethereal* (London, 2010), p. 256.

6 Naomi Mitchison, 'Letters: Gas Masks', *New Scientist* (1975), p. 279.

7 Jean Baudrillard and David Macey (translator), 'Hyperreal America', *Economy and Society*, XXII/2 (May 1993), pp. 243–52 (p. 248).

8 Jean Baudrillard, *The Illusion of the End* (Stanford, CA, 1992), p. 74.

9 Timothy Luke, 'Reproducing Planet Earth? The Hubris of Biosphere 2', *The Ecologist*, XXV/4 (1995), pp. 157–64 (p. 159).

10 Eva Díaz, 'Dome Culture in the 21st Century', *Grey Room*, XLII (Winter 2011), pp. 80–105.

11 The Survivaball model of air architectures is pretty well expressed in *The Wind From Nowhere* (1961), J. G. Ballard's overlooked and modestly self-maligned text about a wind which is destroying most of life on the planet. In Ballard's novel, first published in 1961, the world's only surviving megalomaniac builds a vast pyramid which rises up against the wind storm. This is the home of Hardoon, the 55-year-old millionaire who, like any Bond villain, controls the boundaries with the outside world. He presses a button and turns in his chair (without a cat on his arm) to withdraw the pyramid shutters and reveal the plate glass, 3 feet deep, keeping the winds of the outside at bay. Ballard, apparently embarrassed by first work, would go on to claim that *The Wind From Nowhere* should not count as his first novel, claiming it as a piece of 'hack' work intended solely to be noticed by potential publishers.

12 E. B. White, 'Here is New York', in *Empire City: New York through the Ages* (New York, 2005), p. 710.

13 Ibid., p. 710.

14 Ibid., p. 697.

15 Ibid., p. 696.

16 Ibid., p. 697.

17 The United States and the United Nations, 'Report by the President to the Congress for the Year 1947', *Department of State Publication 3024*, International Organization and Conference Series III, (Washington, DC), p. 220.

18 Le Corbusier quoted in Michael Raeburn and Victoria Wilson, eds, *Le Corbusier: Architect of the Century*, exh. cat., Hayward Gallery, London (1987), p. 170.

19 H.A.P. Kliban, 'Pinch and Punch', *Architectural Visions of the United Nations* (Cambridge, 1949).

20 See the excellent analysis of the ventilation debate by J. Hiller and S. J. Bell, 'The 'Genius of Place': Mitigating Stench in the New Palace of Westminster before the Great Stink', *The London Journal*, XXXV/1 (2010), pp. 22–38.

21 David Boswell Reid, *Illustrations on the Theory and Practice of Ventilation: With Remarks on the Warming, Exclusive Lighting and the Communication of Sound* (London, 1844), p. xiii.

22 Paulo Tavares, *General Essay on Air: Probes into the Atmospheric Conditions of Liberal Democracy* (London, 2008).

23 Communications passed to Viscount Duncannon explained that the air was impregnated by the dust and mud from members' feet. Sir F. Trench to Viscount Duncannon, House of Commons Parliamentary Papers, No. 204, Sessions 1838: http://parlipapers.chadwyck.co.uk.

24 Reid, *Illustrations*, p. 274.

25 Editorial, *London Quarterly Review* (1846), p. 316.

26 Both Lord Sudely and Benjamin Hawes were quoted in David Boswell Reid and Elisha Harris, *Ventilation in America: With a Series of Diagrams, Presenting Examples in Different Classes of Habitations* (New York, 1864), p. xxv.

27 Editorial, p. 214.

28 Reid's work was published in the U.S. as *Ventilation in American Dwellings* by David Boswell Reid and Elisha Harris (1858). See also E. Harris, 'Vital Registration – Public Use of Vital Statistics', *New York Times* (23 May 1874).

29 Edwin Chadwick, 'Ventilation with Air', *The Sanitarian* (1885), p. 13.

30 Vladimir Jankovic and Michael Hebbert, 'Hidden Climate Change: Urban Meteorology and the Scales of Real Weather', *Climatic Change*, 113 (2012), pp. 23–33.

31 Rudyard Kipling, *Plain Tales from the Hills* (London, 1888 [repr. 2011]).

32 Dane Kennedy, *The Magic Mountains: Hill Stations and the British Raj* (Los Angeles, 1996).

33 David Gilmour, *The Ruling Caste: Imperial Lives in the Victorian Raj* (London, 2007), p. 269.

34 Mollie Panter-Downes, *Ooty Preserved: A Victorian Hill Station in India* (London, 1967), p. 8.

35 Judith T. Kenny, 'Climate, Race, and Imperial Authority: The Symbolic Landscape of the British Hill Station in India', *Annals of the Association of American Geographers*, LXXXV/4 (December 1995), pp. 694–714 (p. 699).

36 Kavita Philip, 'English Mud: Towards a Critical Cultural Studies of Colonial Science', *Cultural Studies*, XII/3 (1 July 1998), pp. 300–31 (p. 304).

37 Georgina Gowans, 'Imperial Geographies of Home: Memsahibs and Miss-Sahibs2 in India and Britain, 1915–1947', *Cultural Geographies*, X/4 (2003), pp. 424–41 (p. 431).

38 Ibid., p. 433.

39 Anita Desai, 'Hill Stations of the Raj', *New York Times*, www.nytimes.com, 15 March 1987.

40 D. Asher Ghertner, 'Calculating Without Numbers: Aesthetic
    Governmentality in Delhi's Slums', *Economy and Society*, XXXIX/2
    (2010), pp. 185–217.
41 Colin McFarlane, 'The Politics of Open Defecation: Informality,
    Body and Infrastructure in Mumbai' (working paper, 2011).
42 I am grateful for having heard the fascinating talk by the UCL
    geographer Andrew Harris who pointed out this moment in
    Slumdog Millionaire. Andrew Harris, 'Vertical Urbanism',
    Vertical Geographies workshop, London, 8 December 2010:
    http://backdoorbroadcasting.net.
43 Cited in Marsha Ackermann, *Cool Comfort: America's Romance with
    Air-conditioning* (Washington, DC, 2010), p. 157.
44 Lewis Mumford, 'Sketch of the City of the Future', *Survey* (1925).

5 Mirage

1   James Thomson, *The City of Dreadful Night and Other Poems*
    (London, 1880), p. 8.
2   Ellsworth Huntington, *Civilization and Climate* (Honolulu, 2001
    [first published 1915]).
3   Ibid., p. 224.
4   Raymond Arsenault, 'The End of the Long Hot Summer: The Air
    Conditioner and Southern Culture', *The Journal of Southern History*,
    L/4 (November 1984), pp. 597–628.
5   T. E. Lawrence, *Oriental Assembly* (London, 2005), p. 12.
6   Robert Southey, *Thalaba the Destroyer* (London, 1801), p. 28.
7   Stan Cox, 'Militarism, Torture . . . and Air Conditioning',
    www.counterpunch.org/2010/04/22.
8   Graeme Wood, 'An Air-conditioned Nightmare', *The Atlantic*,
    www.theatlantic.com, 14 August 2008.
9   Jeremy Bernstein, 'That "Sweet Abbottabad Air"', *New York Review
    of Books*, www.nybooks.com, 5 May 2011.
10 Aravind Adiga, *The White Tiger* (New York and London, 2008),
    p. 137.
11 Ibid., pp. 132–4.
12 Joshua Apte et al., 'Concentrations of Fine, Ultrafine, and
    Black Carbon Particles in Auto-rickshaws in New Delhi, India',
    Atmospheric Environment, XLV/26 (2011), pp. 4470–80.
13 Bret Easton Ellis, *American Psycho* (New York, 1991), p. 152.
14 Sherman also works for Pierce & Pierce, that is, the same
    investment firm as Bateman.
15 Tom Wolfe, *Bonfire of the Vanities* (New York, 2003), p. 56.
16 Jonathan Raban, *Hunting Mister Heartbreak* (New York, 1991), p. 81.
17 Ibid., p. 87.

18 Wolfe, *Bonfire*, p. 536.
19 Friedrich Nietzsche, *Ecce Homo*, trans. Duncan Large (Oxford, 2007).
20 Ibid., p. 17.
21 *All Quiet on the Western Front* [1929], trans. Brian Murdoch (New York, 1996) p. 148.
22 Ibid., p. 151.
23 Darius Rejali, 'Ice Water and Sweatboxes: The Long and Sadistic History Behind the CIA's Torture Techniques', *Slate*, www.slate.com, 2009.
24 See Dominique Moran, *Mapping the Gulag*, www.gulagmaps.org.
25 Jameel Jaffer and Amrit Singh, *Administration of Torture: A Documentary Record from Washington to Abu Ghraib and Beyond* (New York, 2007), p. 153.
26 Milica Tomić, 'CONTAINER: Forensic Performance: (Re)Construction of the Crime', http://milicatomic.wordpress.com.
27 Huntingdon, *Civilization*, p. 227.
28 Stephen Healey, 'Air-conditioning and the "Homogenization" of People and Environments', *Building Research and Information* (2008), p. 312.
29 Lisa Heschong, *Thermal Delight in Architecture* (Cambridge, 1979).
30 Madhavi Indraganti, 'Thermal Comfort in Apartments in India: Adaptive Use of Environmental Controls and Hindrances', *Renewable Energy: An International Journal*, XXXVI /4 (April 2011), pp. 1182–9; 'Behavioural Adaptation and the use of Environmental Controls in Summer for Thermal Comfort in Apartments in India', *Energy and Buildings*, XLII (2010), pp. 1019–25.
31 Elizabeth Shove, *Comfort, Cleanliness and Convenience: The Social Organization of Normality* (Oxford, 2003) pp. 50–69.
32 Russell Hitchings and Shu Jun Lee, 'Air-conditioning and the Material Culture of Routine Human Encasement', *Journal of Material Culture*, XIII/3 (2008), pp. 251–65.

6 Dust to Dust

1 Frédéric Beigbeder, *Windows On the World: A Novel*, trans. Frank Wynne (New York, 2004), p. 85.
2 J. G. Ballard, *The Wind From Nowhere* (New York, 1962), pp. 1–10.
3 J. G. Ballard, 'Going Somewhere?', *The Observer* (14 September 1997).
4 See also Christopher Schaberg's tremendous book, *The Textual Life of Airports* (London, 2012).
5 Lily Ford, 'Mapping the Clouds', *Fortean Times*, www.forteantimes.com, May 2010.

6 Carol Ann Duffy, 'Silver Lining', performed by the poet on *Today*, BBC Radio 4, www.bbc.co.uk, 19 April 2010.

7 Val Gielgud, *Death at Broadcasting House* (London, 1934).

8 Carrier Corporation, *An Air Conditioning Achievement by Carrier: Broadcasting House* (London, 1932), p. 2.

9 Quoted in Staffan Ericson, 'The Interior of the Ubiquitous: Broadcasting House, London', in *Media Houses: Architecture, Media and the Production of Centrality* (New York, 2010), pp. 19–58.

10 Herman Klein 'The Genii of Broadcasting House', *The Gramophone and the Singer* (6–7 July 1932), p. 6.

11 Carrier Corporation, *An Air Conditioning Achievement*, p. 10.

12 *Death at Broadcasting House*, dir. Reginald Denham (Phoenix Films, London, 1934).

13 Steven Connor, 'The Machine in the Ghost: Spiritualism, Technology and the "Direct Voice"', in *Ghosts: Deconstruction, Psychoanalysis, History*, ed. Peter Buse and Andrew Stott (Basingstoke, 1999), pp. 203–25 (p. 211).

14 Julian Barnes, *Arthur and George* (London, 2006); Arthur Conan Doyle, *The Poison Belt* (London, 1913).

15 Susan Hill, *The Woman in Black* (London, 1983); see also, particularly, Henning Mankell, *The Man who Smiled* (London 2005 [first published 1994]).

16 Diane Jacobs, *Her Own Woman: The Life of Mary Wollstonecraft* (London, 2001), p. 219.

17 The account is also drawn from Godwin's long chapter-length discussion of Mary's suicide attempt in *Memoirs of the Author of A Vindication of the Rights of Women* (London, 1798), p. 138.

18 Helen M. Buss, 'Godwin's Memoirs', in *Writing Lives: Mary Wollstonecraft and Mary Shelley*, ed. Helen M. Buss, D. L. Macdonald and Anne McWhir (Waterloo, ON, 2001), p. 122.

19 Carolyn Williams, '"Inhumanly Brought Back to Life and Misery": Mary Wollstonecraft, Frankenstein, and the Royal Humane Society', *Women's Writing*, VIII/2 (2001), pp. 213–34 (p. 223).

20 See Diana Coke's instructive and detailed history of the Royal Humane Society, *Saved From a Watery Grave* (London, 1998), p. 2.

21 A. Barrington Baker, 'Artificial Respiration, the History of an Idea', *Journal of Medical History*, XV (1971), pp. 336–51 (p. 336).

22 C.P.F. O'Donnell, A. T. Gibson and P. G. Davis, 'Pinching, Electrocution, Ravens' Beaks, and Positive Pressure Ventilation: A Brief History of Neonatal Resuscitation', *Archives of Disease in Childhood, Fetal and Neonatal Edition*, XCI/5 (2006), pp. 369–73 (p. 370).

23 John Fothergill, 'Observations of a Case Published in the Last

Volume of the *Medical Essays*, "of recovering a Man dead in Appearance by distending the lungs with Air'", in *The Works of John Fothergill, M.D.*, vol. 1, ed. J. C. Lettsom (London, 1783), p. 278.

24 'Royal Humane Society', *The Gentleman's Magazine* (1821), p. 807.

25 O'Donnell et al., 'Pinching', p. 370.

26 Roger Ingpen, *Shelley in England: New Facts and Letters from the Shelley-Witton Papers* (London, 1917), p. 476.

27 Sara Wasson, *Urban Gothic of the Second World War* (Basingstoke, 2010), p. 8.

28 Bao Ninh, *The Sorrow of War* (New York, 1994), pp. 21–2.

29 Ibid., p. 78.

30 Ibid., p. 99.

31 J. G. Ballard, *Empire of the Sun* (London, 1984), p. 30.

32 Beigbeder, *Windows*, p. 60.

33 Martin Amis, *The Second Plane* (London, 2008), pp. 1–3.

34 Ibid., p. 6.

35 Ian Cook et al., 'Hartmut Bitomsky's *Dust*': A Reaction More than a Review', *Science as Culture*, XX/1 (March 2011), p. 117.

36 Paul J. Lioy, *Dust: The Inside Story of its Role in the September 11th Aftermath* (Lanham, MD, 2010), p. 44.

37 Goyard had been a stage designer and stage decorator in both Belgium and France. In 1934, he designed the scenery for *Les Races* at the Théâtre de L'Oeuvre in the rue de Clichy. The play was particularly critical of National Socialism and its anti-Semitic posture.

38 Celan cited in Gary D. Mole, *Beyond the Limit-experience: French Poetry of the Deportation, 1940–1945* (New York, 2002), p. 168.

39 Edward Abbey, *Confessions of a Barbarian: Selections of the Journals of Edward Abbey* (London, 2003).

40 I am grateful to Regina Ammicht-Quinn for pointing out Nicolas Berg's *Luftmenschen: Zur Geschichte einer Metapher* (Göttigen, 2008).

41 This is the phrase used by poet and songwriter Wolf Biermann remembering the awful scenes of the firestorm that swept Hamburg at the hands of Allied bombers on the night of 27 July 1943. This is taken from Keith Lowe's incredible book, *Inferno* (London, 2009).

42 Abbey, *Confessions*, pp. 89–90.

43 Philip Pullman, *The Amber Spyglass: His Dark Materials* (London, 2005), p. 455.

44 Luce Irigaray, *The Forgetting of Air in Martin Heidegger* (Austin, TX, 1999).

45 Don DeLillo, 'In the Ruins of the Future: Reflections on the Terror and Loss in the Shadow of September', *Harper's Magazine* (December 2001).

SELECT BIBLIOGRAPHY

Ackermann, Marsha, *Cool Comfort: America's Romance with
  Air-Conditioning* (Washington, DC, and London, 2010)
Adey, Peter, *Aerial Life* (London 2010)
Adiga, Aravind, *The White Tiger* (New York and London, 2008)
Bachelard, Gaston, *Air and Dreams; An Essay on the Imagination of
  Movement* (Dallas, TX, 1988)
Ballard, J. G., *Empire of the Sun* (London, 1984)
Barnes, David S., *The Great Stink of Paris and the Nineteenth-century
  Struggle against Filth and Germs* (Baltimore, MD, 2006)
Berman, Marshall, *All that is Solid Melts into Air* (New York, 1983)
Boswell-Reid, David. *Illustrations on the Theory and Practice of Ventilation:
  with remarks on the warming, exclusive lighting and the communication
  of sound* (London, 1844)
Burton, Robert, *The Anatomy of Melancholy* (New York, 1870)
Cockayne, Emily, *Hubbub: Filth, Noise and Stench in England*,
  (Ann Arbor, MI, 2007)
Coke, Diana, *Saved from a Watery Grave* (London, 1998)
Connor, Steven, *The Matter of Air* (London, 2010)
Corbin, Alain, *The Lure of the Sea* (Los Angeles, 1994)
Corn, Joseph, *The Winged Gospel* (Washington, DC, 1993)
Ellis, Bret Easton, *American Psycho* (New York, 1991)
Gaskell, Elizabeth, *North and South* [1855] (London, 2003)
Gissen, David, *Subnature: Architecture's other Environments*
  (London, 2009)
——, 'The Architectural Production of Nature/New York', in
  Grey Room (Winter 2009) pp. 58–79
Goodman, Martin, *Suffer and Survive: The Extreme Life of J. S. Haldane*,
  (London, 2007)
Hamblyn, Richard, *The Invention of Clouds: How an Amateur
  Meteorologist Formed the Language of the Skies* (New York, 2001)

Howard, Luke, *The Climate of London,* (London 1833)

Huntington, Ellsworth, *Civilisation and Climate* (Hawaii, 2001)

Irigaray, Luce, *The Forgetting of Air in Martin Heidegger*
    (Austin, TX, 1999)

Jankovic, Vladimir, *Reading the Skies: A Cultural History of English
    Weather, 1650–1820* (Chicago, 2001)

Johnson, Stephen, *The Invention of Air: An Experiment, a Journey,
    a New Country, and the Amazing Force of Scientific Discovery*
    (London, 2009)

Kennedy, Dane, *The Magic Mountains: Hill Stations and the British Raj*
    (Los Angeles, 1996)

Lioy, Paul, *Dust: The Inside Story of its Role in the September 11th
    Aftermath* (Lanham, MD, 2010)

McCormack, Derek P., 'Aerostatic Spacing: on Things Becoming
    Lighter than Air', *Transactions of the Institute of British Geographers*
    (2009)

Overy, Paul, *Light, Air and Openness: Modern Architecture Between the
    Wars* (London, 2008)

Saint-Exupéry, Antoine de, *Southern Mail, Night Flight,* trans Curtis
    Cate (London, 1971)

Schaberg, Christopher, *The Textual Life of Airports: Reading the Culture
    of Flight* (London, 2012)

Schaffer, Simon, 'Measuring Virtue: Eudiometry, Enlightenment,
    and Pneumatic Medicine', in Andrew Cunningham and Roger
    French, eds, *The Medical Enlightenment of the Eighteenth Century*
    (Cambridge, 1990)

Shapin, Stephen, and Simon Schaffer, *Leviathan and the Air-Pump:
    Hobbes, Boyle, and the Experimental Life* (Princeton, NJ, 1985)

Shove, Elizabeth, *Comfort, Cleanliness and Convenience: The Social
    Organisation of Normality* (Oxford, 2003)

Sloterdijk, Peter, *Terror From the Air* (Cambridge, MA, 2008)

——, *Bubbles* (Cambridge, MA, 2011)

Sontag, Susan, *Illness as Metaphor* (London, 1991)

Suskind, Patrick, *Perfume: The Story of a Murderer* (London, 1985)

Uglow, Jenny, *The Lunar Men: The Friends who Made the Future,
    1730–1810* (New York, 2002)

Wasson, Sara, *Urban Gothic of the Second World War* (Basingstoke, 2010)

ASSOCIATIONS AND WEBSITES

The Yes Men have helped raise the profile of a number of vitally important issues involving air and disaster. Their work on the Bhopal poison gas catastrophe and their Surivaball spoof can be found at their website: http://theyesmen.org

China Air Daily is a production by the Asia Society Center on u.s.–China Relations which monitors air pollution and uses innovative methods of air recording and visualisation, including maps and image overlays, and kites flown with webcams attached to them: www.chinaairdaily.com

Bret Holman's Airminded website and blog is by far the world's best resource for the history of air, geopolitics and society. His postings count airships, and colonial air control to the terrible fears over gas attack in the build up to the World War Two: http://airminded.org

Julie Westerman is a Sheffield based artist who works with lots of things airy. From the aerodynamics of shuttle cocks to wind, draughts and an intervention on a soon to be closed Berlin airport, her projects can be found at: www.juliewesterman.co.uk

Berndnaut Smilde's extraordinary works on indoor clouds are collated at his personal website: www.berndnaut.nl

The Royal Humane Society have a fantastically informative website about their origins and current activities. Their records can be accessed at the London Metropolitan Archives: www.royalhumanesociety.org.uk

Paulo Tavares, *General Essay on Air: Probes into the Atmospheric Conditions of Liberal Democracy* (London, 2008), www.paulotavares.net/air

David Gissen's writing on urban natures and the indoor production of manufactured air can be found at his website: http:// htcexperiments. org

Other important websites

www.ipcc.ch
www.metoffice.gov.uk
www.sciencemuseum.org.uk
www.wellcome.ac.uk
www.citiesforcleanair.org
www.cseindia.org

ACKNOWLEDGEMENTS

This book has been incubating for a very long time. My geography and science teachers at Ferndown Middle and Upper Schools, particularly Mrs Dibden and Mr and Mrs Powell, were incredibly supportive of my early interest in the atmosphere and the enveloping gases that surround and protect us. Growing up in the '80s amid new-found holes in the ozone layer was utterly formative, even if this book takes the notion of air in some different and maybe odd directions to those where I first started.

For a short book, this has been quite a labour, and I am appreciative to Daniel Allen, Michael Leaman and Robert Williams at Reaktion for their encouragement and patience and for pushing me to get the book right. I hope *Air* is an example of when good criticism goes a long way.

As always, colleagues and friends have been fantastically supportive, especially as this book was completed following a move from the University of Keele to Royal Holloway. Thanks are particularly due to Klaus Dodds, who read through final drafts at the last minute. Many thanks go to Peter Knight, as we discussed our first ideas together – I'm looking forward to *Glacier*! Usual thanks for thoughts, advice and inspiration go to Ben Anderson, Oliver Belcher, Rachel Colls, Martin Coward, Phil Crang, Tim Cresswell, Steve Graham, Derek Gregory, Harriet Hawkins, Clare Holdsworth, Caren Kaplan, Peter Kraftl, Derek McCormack, Craig Martin, Damien Masson, Patrick Murphy, Kim Peters, Alasdair Pinkerton, Zoe Robinson, Paul Simpson, Rachael Squire, Phil Steinberg, Paulo Tavares, Rich Waller, Mark Whitehead, Alison Williams and Chris Zebrowski. And a special mention must go to Nanna and Grandad Searles for stories about Mundesley, and thanks too for being so persistent about that *Liegehalle* summerhouse!

Lastly, thank you to my wife and family.

PHOTO ACKNOWLEDGEMENTS

The author and publishers wish to express their thanks to the below sources of illustrative material and/or permission to reproduce it. Locations of some artworks are also given below.

Photo afghan diary: p. 158; photos © Matt Allen: pp. 109, 110; © Joshua Apte: p. 160; photos author: pp. 65, 113, 135; © Peter Böhi: p. 94; Andrea Booher, FEMA News Photo: p. 193; photo courtesy of Carl Bourdain: p. 34; The British Museum, London: p. 77; photos © Trustees of the British Museum: pp. 32, 34, 47, 48, 77, 82, 101; from F. W. Burton-Fanning, 'Open Air Treatment of Phithisis in England', © *Lancet* (1898): p. 111; City of Chicago Municipal Tuberculosis Sanitarium, 1915: p. 117; William C. Cooke: p. 99; photo Onur Dag: p. 170; © Catherine D'Ignazio: p. 90 (foot); from *Frank Leslie's Illustrated Newspaper* (27 October 1888): p. 68; © David Gissen: p. 90 (top); from J.J. Grandville, *Un Autre Monde* (Paris, 1844): p. 34; from *Harper's Weekly* (12 February 1876): p. 66; Houston Museum of Natural Science: p. 14; photo courtesy Institute of Mechanical Engineers, London: p. 64; photo John Springer Collection/Corbis: p. 55; © Yves Klein, ADAGP, Paris: pp. 127, 128; from E. H. Knight, *Knight's American Mechanical Dictionary* (New York, 1876): p. 18; from Marsilio Landriani, *Ricerche fisiche intorno alla salubrita dell'aria* (Milan, *c.* 1775): p. 72; from Antoine Lavoisier, *Elements of Chemistry* (London, 1790): p. 22; courtesy of the Lewis Walpole Library, Yale University: p. 44; courtesy of the Library of Congress, Washington, DC: pp. 59, 66, 68, 69, 138, 190; photo (WT-shared) Mr Stew: p. 168; photo © NACA: p. 52; NASA AquaSat: p. 173; National Gallery, London: p. 35; photo National Library of France: p. 29; © National Portrait Gallery, London: pp. 24, 83, 124; photo Nomadsolicitor at English Wikivoyage: p. 195; from *Philosophical Transactions of the Royal Society of London. Series B. Containing Papers of a Biological Character*, 203, pp. 185-318 (1913): pp. 121, 122, 123; © *Postgraduate Medical Journal* (2010): p. 105; *Report from Select Committee on the Ventilation of the Houses of Parliament; with the minutes of evidence*, 573 (1835): p. 140; photo ©

Mike Robbins: p. 126; courtesy of the artist (Berndnaut Smilde) and Ronchini Gallery: p. 170; photo Somjal: p. 189; photo by Rachael Squire: p. 174; from *St Louis Courier of Medicine*, xxxi/ 6 (1904): p. 115; photo by Bill Taub © NACA: p. 53; photo © Tom Little photography: p. 132; © Milica Tomic: p. 167; photo u.s. Department of Defense: pp. 38-9; courtesy u.s. Naval Radiological Defence Laboratory: p. 40; from u.s. Naval Radiological Defence Laboratory [C. E. Adams, J. D. Connor], *The Nature of Individual Radioactive Particles vi. Fallout Particles from a Tower Shot, Operation Redwing* (San Francisco, CA, 1957): p. 40; photo © Nirupa Varatharasan: p. 89; Victoria & Albert Museum, London (photos © the Trustees of the V&A Museum): pp. 74, 146; photos © the Trustees of the V&A Museum, London: pp. 19, 28, 36, 37, 41, 74, 130, 146; © Trustees of the Watts Gallery, Compton, Surrey: p. 186; courtesy Wellcome Library, London: pp. 20, 21, 23, 27, 63, 67, 72, 106, 112, 114, 116, 181, 182, 184, 185.

Jon, the copyright holder of the image on p. 131, has published it online under conditions imposed by a Creative Commons Attribution 2.0 Generic licence; Norbert Aepli, the copyright holder of the image on p. 129, andytang20, the copyright holder of the image on p. 14, and Gopal Aggarwal (www.gopal1035.blogspot.com), the copyright holder of the image on p. 145, have published these online under conditions imposed by a Creative Commons Attribution 2.5 Generic license; and Dkganesh, the copyright holder of the image on p. 62, Ad Meskens/Wikimedia Commons, the copyright holder of the image on p. 155, Krupasindhu Muduli, the copyright holder of the image on p. 148, and Frank Seiplax, the copyright holder of the image on p. 157, have published these online under conditions imposed by a Creative Commons Attribution-Share Alike 3.0 Unported license.

Readers are free:
• to share – to copy, distribute and transmit these images alone
• to remix – to adapt these images alone

Under the following conditions:

• attribution – readers must attribute either image in the manner specified by the author or licensor (but not in any way that suggests that these parties endorse them or their use of the work).
• share alike – If readers alter, transform or build upon this image, they may distribute the resulting work only under the same or similar licence to this one.

INDEX